CW00659498

The Enchanted Sole

Legendary Socks for Adventurous Knitters

Janel Laidman

RUSTLING LEAF PRESS

Text, Photography & Illustrations © 2009 Rustling Leaf Press
Second Edition

Illustrator - Janel Laidman
Photographer - Ben Wheeler
Tech Editors - Amy Polcyn, Jeane DeCoster
Copy Editors - Amy Polcyn, Kathy Hinckley

All rights reserved. No part of this book may be reproduced or transmitted in any form or by any means, electronic or mechanical, including photocopying, recording, or by any other information storage technique, except for inclusion of brief quotations in an article or review, without the express written consent of the author.

Rustling Leaf Press

P.O. Box 21805

Eugene, OR 97402

www.rustlingleafpress.com

Printed in Canada by Friesens

Laidman, Janel, 1963 -
The Enchanted Sole 2009
ISBN 978-0-9814972-3-5

RUSTLING LEAF PRESS

for Bryce and Wilma who have always nurtured my dreams

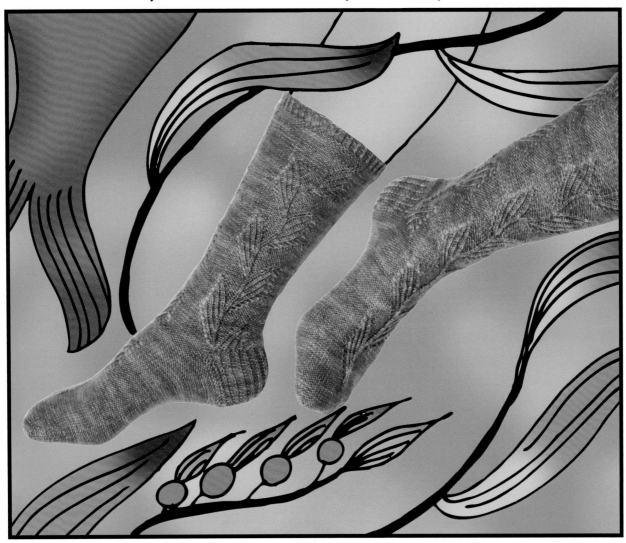

and for Rustle, always for Rustle

In Gratitude Whereof:

I am indebted to many people who helped make this book a reality.

As always, I owe Cat Bordhi my heartfelt thanks for her generosity of spirit, sage advice and unfailing support, and my pattern writing mentors Cookie A. and Anne Hanson who helped me see the error of my ways.

A big thanks goes to Ben Wheeler for his beautiful photography, his cheerful jokes when sessions ran late and his creative suggestions, and to Bridget Landry and Inna Pashkov for their beautiful feet, their enthusiasm and suggestions for modeling shots and their willingness to assume the most unnatural poses in the quest of looking natural.

I owe a big debt of gratitude to my two technical editors who took the raw patterns and helped me make them something useable. Thanks and hugs to Amy Polcyn and Jeane DeCoster. Special thanks to Kathy Hinckley for her copy editing help.

A huge THANK YOU! to all of the sample knitters who did such a lovely job of making my designs a reality.

Jennifer Adams	Daniel Herrera
Cathy Berry	Natalie Jacobs
Jeannie Cartmel	Sarah Kirschling
Karen Fraser	Bridget Landry
Erika Grant	Jenny Prokopovich
Georg Hawks	Stormy Tetreault
Tabetha Hedrick	Harriet Wintermute

I must also thank all of my fantastic test knitters who test drove the patterns and provided such valuable feedback.

Constance M. Cole	Carla Willingham	Robbin L. Koenig
Evelyn Rector	Heidi Rae Porter	Ellen Hogan
Katrina Cunningham	MaryAnn Sims	Lynne Evans
Andrea Sinclair	Amy Hoover	Lise Brackbill
Rachel Horsting	Cathy Berry	Maxine How
Anna Koop	Courtney Opheim	Dorothy Dean
Christine Babron	Barb Goldhamer	Phyllis G. Lederman
Jennifer D. Rice		

Special thanks go to Kimley Maretzo, JC Briar, Chris DeLongpre and members of the Visionary Self Publishing group for their support of me and their critical eyes. I am always grateful to Deb Robson for her lovely advice and wonderful example.

And of course, my loving husband Russell without whom none of this would make sense and my family who have always supported my dreams.

Thank you all.

Contents

Introduction

Socks make such a wonderful small canvas to try out design ideas. Each sock pattern in this collection began as an inspiration; an inspiration from the yarn, the story, or a stitch pattern. The techniques are varied; however, each pattern is related to the overall theme of myth, legend and fairy tale. Each pattern was an adventure for me to create, and I hope it will be a knitting adventure for you as well.

Swatching and Gauge.

Socks are small projects. Often just beginning the sock is enough swatching to carry on with the knitting of the sock. Check your gauge as you begin and adjust when necessary. Some sock constructions require a closer attention to gauge. In general, the more elastic a sock stitch pattern is, the less important gauge is. However, gauge is particularly important in the sideways socks and the colorwork socks. With sideways socks you will need to know both your stitch and row gauge in order to achieve a good fit. With colorwork socks, you have less elasticity, so your finished, relaxed circumference of the sock needs to be closer to the actual circumference measurement of your leg.

If you will be knitting your sock in the round, either on DPNs or circular needles, you should swatch in the round with those needles. Likewise, if you are knitting a sock flat, like the sideways construction method, you will want to swatch flat.

As always, the needle size recommended in a particular pattern is just that, a recommendation. If you are not achieving the correct gauge with that needle size, change needle sizes and/or yarn sizes until you achieve the gauge you want.

Yarn and Fibers

Each pattern carries an information box with the particulars of the yarns used in the models depicted in the book. This information should help you source the same yarns or find suitable yarns to substitute.

The yarn specs carry a category titled WPI. This stands for wraps per inch, and is a method of gauging the *grist* or thickness of a yarn. It is a more accurate method for subsitution because yarn weight is an obscure method of description rooted in archaic industrial practices. To determine the WPI of a yarn you are thinking of using, wrap the yarn around a ruler or other gauge marked out in inches. The wraps should just touch each other without crowding or gaps. The number of times you can wrap around the ruler in one inch is the WPI number.

Needle Choices - DPNs or Circulars?

All of the patterns in the book can be knit on either double pointed needles (DPNs) or circular needles in the case of the socks knit in the round and either straight or circular needles in the case of the socks knit flat from the side. Each pattern has designated instep stitches and heel stitches, or inside stitches and outside stitches.

You can divide these stitches onto DPNs, one circular or two circulars according to your preference. Stitch counts are given frequently to help you keep track of where the stitches should be. If you are using DPNs, I usually recommend dividing the instep stitches on 2 needles and the heel stitches on 2 needles and using a fifth needle to knit. If you prefer magic loop, it will probably be easiest if instep stitches are on one side of the loop and heel stitches on the other. Likewise, if you use the two circulars method, instep stitches should go on one circular needle and heel stitches on the other. If you have trouble keeping track of where your instep stitches and heel stitches are, markers can be helpful.

Colors

All of the patterns have recommendations for color choices when substituting yarns. A solid color is one that has probably been commercially dyed and is without variation. Solid colors will give you the most stitch definition. A semi-solid color is usually hand dyed, although you may find commercial examples as well. A semi-solid is a color in which the hue stays the same but there are changes in value, giving more depth to the color. A semi-solid is a good compromise if you like the stitch definition of a solid, but the soulfulness of a hand dyed yarn. Some semi-solid colors have very subtle variation, and others have a bolder variation. The bigger the value difference from the lightest to the darkest part of the yarn, the busier the yarn will appear.

A painted yarn is one that has several different colors in it. Painted yarns can be striping or random. A painted yarn can be dynamic and exciting with the right pattern, or it can muddy the effect if it fights with the stitch pattern. Painted yarns look especially exciting in sideways constructed socks because striping occurs vertically on the leg instead of around the circumference. In addition, pooling is usually minimized in a sideways sock construction because the modulus of the color repeat is quite different with that construction.

Painted yarns can be combined with solid yarns in stranded colorwork socks for a beautiful artistic effect. When choosing colors for a colorwork sock, it is a good idea to make sure that at least one color is a solid or semi-solid, and that the two colors have enough contrast so that the pattern can read well.

The color recommendations are only suggestions. The socks are your statement, and your color choices will reflect your personality in the socks.

Sizing and Fit

All of the models made for the book are based on a size 7 women's foot and a medium size ankle and calf. Some of the socks have separate sizes given, while others are only one size. If you need to change the size of a sock that is only given in one size you will have to change your needle and yarn size to accommodate the gauge you will need. In general, if you need the sock to come out bigger, you will want *fewer* stitches per inch, and if you want the sock to come out smaller, you will want *more* stitches per inch.

For each sock, circumference measurements are given. The length measurements are variable and are determined by you based on your foot length. The circumference measurements are given for the sock in its *unstretched* state. The sock will stretch to accommodate a larger circumference. To determine the right circumference for you, I recommend measuring your foot and ankle circumference and choosing one of the sizes offered that is closest to your circumference without going over. As you begin to knit the sock, try it on your foot and make sure it fits over your heel before you progress too far. If the fit is off, choose another size or adjust your gauge as necessary.

Many of the socks in this book have some sort of calf shaping built into the pattern. For a sock knit in the round this will be in the form of increases if the sock is knit toe up or decreases if it is knit top down. You can usually add more or fewer increases or decreases to help with size and fit by determining the increase or decrease pattern in the sock and adjusting accordingly.

Two types of socks in this book have special fit considerations; the sideways constructed socks and the colorwork socks. For sideways constructed socks it is very important to know both your stitch gauge and your row gauge. Your stitch gauge will tell you how many stitches you need to cast on, and your row gauge will determine your circumference. For more about sideways construction fit, see the section on sideways socks.

Because of the nature of stranded knitting, colorwork socks have less elasticity than many other types of stitch patterns used in socks. It is important with colorwork socks that your unstretched circumference be close to your actual circumference, and that shaping is built into the sock. For more about colorwork construction and fit, see the section on colorwork.

I have given sizing tips at the beginning of each pattern to let you know whether you will need to adjust your gauge to achieve different sock sizes.

It is always best to take the actual measurements of your foot, but I have included here a chart of approximate sizes based on shoe sizes for guesstimation purposes, in the event you are unable to measure the actual foot.

Women's Shoe Size	Approximate Foot Length (inches)	Approximate Ball and Ankle Circumference (inches)	Men's Shoe Size	Approximate Foot Length (inches)	Approximiate Ball and Ankle Circumference (inches)
4	8.5	8.25	5	9.25	9.0
5	8.75	8.5	6	9.5	9.0
6	9.0	9.0	7	10.0	9.25
7	9.5	9.25	8	10.25	9.5
8	9.75	9.5	9	10.5	9.5
9	10.0	9.5	10	11.0	9.75
10	10.5	9.5	11	11.25	10.0
11	10.75	9.75	12	11.5	10.0
12	11.0	10	13	12.0	10.25
13	11.5	10	14	12.5	10.5

Cast Ons and Bind Offs

I have included my favorite, the slip knot cast on, in the glossary of this book. I *unvented* this cast on as a young girl when I was trying to learn the long tail cast on. I like this cast on because it doesn't require a long tail, it is very elastic, and it does not have a discernible front or back to it. It has a clean edge that looks like purl bumps from all angles. You may use any cast on you like for top down socks, keeping in mind that you want your cast on edge to remain elastic. If your chosen cast on is not particularly flexible, you can cast on with a larger size needle, then switch to the correct size to give you gauge.

For toe up socks, I have specified the figure 8 cast on which is included in the glossary of this book. If you have another toe up cast on that you prefer, feel free to use it.

For sideways socks you will need a provisional cast on. I recommend the crochet cast on which is included in the glossary of this book. This cast on is quick and easy to undo when you need to take it out. If you are using it as a provisional cast on, I recommend leaving a little tail as shown in the pictures in the glossary so that you will know which end to undo and pull to unzip the crochet.

For toe up socks I recommend Elizabeth Zimmermann's sewn bind off which is included in the glossary of this book. This bind off is easy to do and creates a clean, flexible, edge that has no discernible front or back, similar to the slip knot cast on. Do not pull your sewn stitches too tight as you want your cast off edge to remain elastic. If you prefer to use another bind off, you can bind off with a larger needle to help keep the edge elastic.

All top down and sideways socks will require some grafting using Kitchener stitch. Instructions for Kitchener stitch are included in the glossary of this book.

Sideways Sock Construction

Sideways socks are knit flat from side to side. This construction has several factors that need to be considered. To get an accurate fit, you must measure both your stitch gauge and your row gauge. Your stitch gauge will help you determine how many stitches to cast on. In the beginning of each sideways pattern there is a worksheet to help you determine the number of stitches to cast on, based on the length of your foot and the gauge specified in the pattern.

Because the socks are knit in the opposite orientation from a sock knit in the round, they are stretchier in length than they are in circumference. Therefore, you will want a little bit more negative ease with a sideways knit sock than you might want with a sock knit in the round. I have estimated a 1" negative ease in the socks, you may want to increase or decrease that amount after you have tried a sideways sock.

Your row gauge will determine how many rows you need to knit to make it around your foot. Because there is less stretch in that dimension than in a traditionally knitted sock, you will want to be pretty accurate with your row gauge. The stitch patterns I have chosen for the sideways sock help build in extra elasticity to help give compression and stretch.

In addition, most of the sideways socks have calf and toe shaping in the form of short rows. To increase or decrease the circumference of the sock you can increase or decrease the short rows.

Colorwork Socks

Colorwork socks are a lot of fun to knit because it is exciting to see the pattern emerging as you go. When working stranded colorwork, it is important to keep your tension tight enough for neat stitches, yet loose enough to have some stretch in the resulting fabric. Because colorwork socks have less elasticity than conventional socks, shaping is built in to all the colorwork socks in this book.

You can work the stranded colorwork one handed or two handed, whichever is most comfortable for you. It is best to avoid dropping and picking up each yarn if possible, as that gives sloppy tension. Instead, try holding one color in each hand and knitting using both picking and throwing methods, or carry both yarns in one hand, alternating as necessary.

When choosing yarns for colorwork socks it is best to choose yarns that have a similar grist and twist so that one yarn does not dominate over the other. Colors should be chosen to contrast well so that the pattern can be seen. I recommend that at least one of the yarns in the colorwork pattern be a solid or semi-solid unless you have extremely good contrast between the yarns.

Should you need to change the shaping on a colorwork pattern, add stitches to, or subtract stitches from, the outer edges of the chart. You can extend the pattern if necessary, or take a few stitches out, keeping in mind the decrease pattern at the edges. Because the socks have less elasticity, the fit feels different on your ankle and calf and you'll have less compression than you would with a sock with ribbing; however, the sturdy nature of the thicker fabric created by stranded colorwork will help the sock stay up on your leg.

If a float is particularly long in a stranded colorwork sock, you may choose to twist the yarns around each other while carrying the float to help anchor it on the back. My personal preference is not to twist floats for any float less than 10 stitches. I find that after one washing the floats stick together fairly well even with superwash yarn, and do not snag. You should twist floats when you feel comfortable with it. There several ways to twist a float, the simplest is to drop the current yarn under the floating yarn, then pick it up again over the floating yarn, catching the float in with the working yarn.

13

Heels

All of the toe up and top down socks in this book have flap and gusset heels. Top down socks have a conventional flap and gusset construction. Toe up socks have two different types of flap and gusset heels, a wide heel as depicted in the Tintagel and Lothlorien patterns, or a narrow heel as described in the Atlantis, Changeling and Galadriel patterns.

If one of these types of heels does not fit your foot well, you can substitute the other type. In addition, although directions are not given for it, you could substitute a short row heel in most of the patterns.

Sideways socks also have two heel constructions. The heel is formed by paired increases until the maximum width is reached, followed by paired decreases until all of the extra stitches have been reduced. One type of heel construction has the paired increases (and decreases) happening every row, creating a 45 degree miter down the center of the side of the heel as in the Talking Fish pattern. The other heel construction has increases (and decreases) happening every other row to form two wedge-shaped areas of increase in the heel as in the Tinker and Naiad patterns. These heels are equally effective and can be easily substituted between patterns.

Reading Charts

Charts are read from the bottom right corner, moving left and upward. All charts show all rows, and show the front side of the stitch, i.e. if the chart shows a knit stitch, it means it is a knit on the right side and purl on the wrong side. This only comes into play in the sideways constructed socks, as socks knit in the round are always knit from the front side. Chart symbol keys are included in each pattern and are also listed in the glossary at the back of the book.

Some charts, by necessity, are quite large, making the reading of them a little strenuous. Feel free to photocopy and enlarge the charts in this book for your own personal use. Please do not photocopy and distribute the charts to others.

Beads

Several patterns in the book call for beads. When choosing beads for a sock, you need to make sure that the hole in the bead is large enough for the yarn to fit through. If you are using seed beads, size 6/0 is a good size to use. Choose beads that contrast well with your yarn if you want them to stand out.

There are two different methods of attaching beads specified, inline bead placement and crochet hook bead placement. With inline bead placement you will need to string all the beads onto the yarn to begin with and move the beads out of the way as you knit until you are ready to place a bead. With this method, beads are placed in between stitches.

The crochet hook bead placement method allows you to place the beads as you knit without stringing them on the yarn first. As you come to a stitch where a bead is to be placed, you place a bead on a small crochet hook, then pull the stitch through the hole in the bead with the hook. With this method you are placing the beads directly onto a stitch.

Myths, Legends and Illustrations

Artistic license has been taken with description of the myths and legends and in the depiction of the socks with the illustrations. This book is not a scholarly approach to folklore, but is, rather, inspired by it. I hope you enjoy the inspiration from the world of fantasy as much as I did.

Let the journey begin!

Recipes for The Socks

Tintagel

*ocated on a windswept coast in Cornwall, Tintagel is the name of the the castle where, legend has it, King Arthur was born to Uther Pendragon. These socks are elegant enough to have been worn by Igraine, Duchess of Cornwall, and mother to the legendary king. And now, you too can dress your feet in royal finery.*

Cast On

Using smaller needle size, cast on 24 stitches using the figure 8 cast on (12 loops = 24 stitches), K 1 round.

Stitches are divided into two groups, instep stitches and heel stitches. (12 stitches each).

Toe

Round 1

    Instep stitches: K

    Heel stitches: K

Round 2

    Instep stitches: K1, M1, K to one stitch before end of instep stitches, M1, K1.

    Heel stitches: Repeat instep stitches.

Repeat Rounds 1 and 2 until you have 64 (68, 72) stitches total; 32 (34, 36) in each group.

Foot

Continue to work each round in stockinette until sock measures 4.75 inches less than total foot length.

Pattern Notes

Finished Circumference Measurements (un-stretched):

	foot	ankle	mid calf
small	7.5 in	7.0 in	8.5 in
medium	8.0 in	8.0 in	8.9 in
large	8.5 in	8.5 in	9.4 in

Yarn Used: Woolen Rabbit **Harmony Sock** (merino/nylon), color "*mad about saffron*", 400 yards, 3.5 oz, 1 skein.

WPI: 15

Needles: DPNs or circulars in size to give correct gauge (2.75 mm –US size 2 suggested), needles one size larger (3.25 mm – US size 3 suggested).

Gauge: 8.5 stitches / 12 rows per inch in stockinette knit in round.

Notions: 2 markers, 52 beads, cable needle, tapestry needle. Beads used here: Crystazzi Round 4mm pearl ecru.

Color Suggestions: Solid or semi-solid colors.

Sizing Notes: Length of foot is measured by trying on sock. This pattern is one size in circumference. To change sizes, increase or decrease needle size and yarn weight to get a different gauge.

GUSSET

Place markers

   Instep stitches: K

   Heel stitches: K1, place Marker 1, M1, K to one stitch before last heel stitch, M1, place Marker 2, K1.

Round 1

   Instep stitches: K

   Heel stitches: K1, M1, K to Marker 1, slip marker, K to Marker 2, slip marker, K to 1 stitch before last heel stitch, M1, K1.

Round 2

   Instep stitches: K

   Heel stitches: K

Repeat Rounds 1 and 2 of gusset formation until you have 16 stitches before Marker 1 and after Marker 2

HEEL

Turn heel

The heel turn is worked only on the heel stitches (between the markers), excluding the gusset stitches.

Row 1

   Work first 16 st of heel stitches to Marker 1. Slip marker.

   K until 1 stitch is left unworked before Marker 2. Wrap the next stitch. Turn your work.

Row 2

   P across until one stitch is left unworked before marker. Wrap the next stitch. Turn your work.

Row 3

   K until 1 stitch is left unworked before wrapped stitch. Wrap the next stitch. Turn your work.

Row 4

   P until 1 stitch is left unworked before wrapped stitch. Wrap the next stitch. Turn your work.

Repeat Rows 3 and 4 until you have 8 wrapped stitches on either end and 14 (16, 18) live stitches in the middle.

Finish heel turn

Row 1

   K all live stitches to the first wrapped stitch. Pick up the stitch and the wrap and knit them together. Pick up the next wrapped stitch and the wrap and knit them together. Continue to pick up wrapped stitches and wraps and knit together until you reach the marker. Turn your work.

Row 2

Slip the first stitch. P across to the first wrapped stitch. Pick up wrapped stitch and the wrap and purl together. Continue to pick up wrapped stitches and wraps and purl together until you reach the marker. Turn your work.

Pick up heel flap

Row 1

Slip first stitch. K to one stitch before last marker. SSK last stitch before marker and first stitch after marker together. You will have to move the marker one stitch to left to avoid trapping the marker. Turn your work.

Row 2

Slip first stitch, P to one stitch before last marker. P last stitch before marker and first stitch after marker together. You will have to move the marker one stitch to left to avoid trapping the marker. Turn your work.

Repeat Rows 1 and 2 until all gusset stitches have been picked up. You should now have 32 (34, 36) heel stitches and 32 (34, 36) instep stitches.

Cuff

Notes:

Beads: *The cuff may be knit with or without beads. If you are knitting with beads, you will need to break the yarn before beginning the cuff. Then, string 26 beads onto your yarn before rejoining to your knitting. As you reach the spot in the pattern where a bead is indicated, slide a bead up the yarn, all the way to the needles, then continue knitting. For more detailed instructions see page 120.*

For small size: *Use the stitches within the black frame on the side panel and the black frame on the front/back panel.*

For medium size: *Use the stitches within the red frame on the side panel and the black frame on the front/back panel.*

For large size: *Use the stitches within the red frame on the side panel and the blue frame on the front/back panel.*

All sizes: *Use the stitches on the increase panels.*

Rearrange stitches to allow for side cables:

Switch to larger needle size and rearrange stitches.

Move last 7 (8, 8) stitches of heel stitches to instep stitches.

Move last 7 (8, 8) stitches of instep stitches to heel stitches.

Each set of stitches includes a side panel, followed by a front/back panel.

Begin Chart 1:

For both sets of stitches, follow Chart 1. When Chart 1 is completed, begin bind off.

Bind Off

Round 1

For small size

Instep stitches: P1, place bead, P1, M1P, P2, place bead. *P5, place bead. Repeat from * once. P2, M1P, P1, place bead. *P5, place bead. Repeat from * 3 more times, end with P4.

Heel stitches: Repeat instep stitches.

For medium size

Instep stitches: P1, place bead, *P5, place bead. Repeat from *, end with P4.

Heel stitches: Repeat instep stitches.

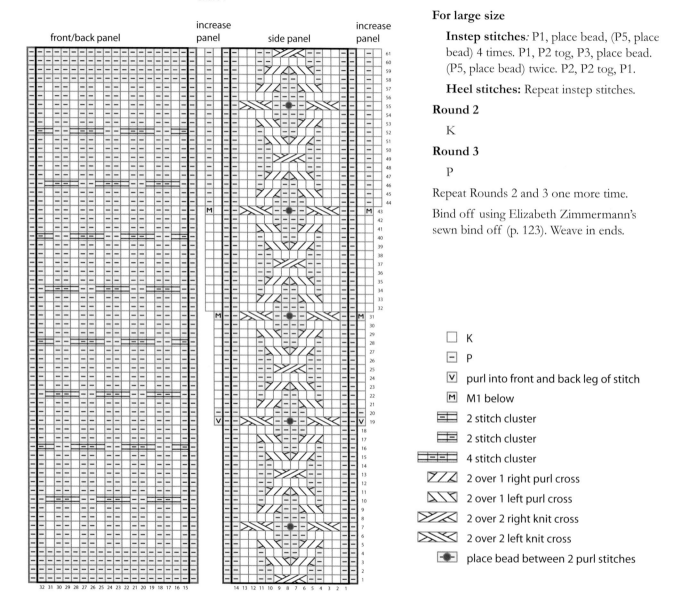

Chart 1

front/back panel

increase panel

side panel

increase panel

For large size

Instep stitches: P1, place bead, (P5, place bead) 4 times. P1, P2 tog, P3, place bead. (P5, place bead) twice. P2, P2 tog, P1.

Heel stitches: Repeat instep stitches.

Round 2

K

Round 3

P

Repeat Rounds 2 and 3 one more time.

Bind off using Elizabeth Zimmermann's sewn bind off (p. 123). Weave in ends.

☐ K

⊟ P

Ⅴ purl into front and back leg of stitch

Ⅿ M1 below

2 stitch cluster

2 stitch cluster

4 stitch cluster

2 over 1 right purl cross

2 over 1 left purl cross

2 over 2 right knit cross

2 over 2 left knit cross

place bead between 2 purl stitches

Labyrinth

urn and turn again. The labyrinth draws you deeper into its heart before it lets you go. These socks remind us of the mystery of the labyrinth as the pattern is slowly revealed while you knit. Make yourself some labyrinth socks when you feel the mood for quiet contemplation and deepening mystery.

Cast On

Cast on 68 stitches in color A and join in the round, taking care not to twist your stitches.

Cuff

Ribbing:

Work 6 rounds of K2 tbl, P2 ribbing in color A.

Set up round:

K 1 round increasing evenly by 12 stitches. You now have 80 stitches.

Begin Chart 1

Work following Chart 1. The beginning of each row is in the center of the heel stitches.

When Chart 1 is completed, begin heel. You should have 68 stitches.

Heel

Set up round:

Rearrange stitches to make 2 sets of stitches, instep stitches and heel stitches. Stitches 1-17 are heel stitches. Stitches 18-52 are instep stitches. Stitches 53-68 are heel stitches.

You should have 35 instep stitches and 33 heel stitches.

Heel flap:

Working only the heel stitches, always slipping the first stitch of each row, and working back and forth, follow Chart 2. When Chart 2 is completed, turn heel.

Pattern Notes

Finished Circumference Measurements (unstretched):

foot	ankle	calf
8.25 in	8.5 in	10.0 in

Yarn Used: Blue and Caramel version: Shibui **Sock** (superwash merino) in color "*honey 1395*" (color A), 191 yards, 1.75 oz, 2 skeins and Pagewood Farm **St. Elias** (Bluefaced Leicester) in color "*peaceful*" (color B), 450 yards, 4 oz, 1 skein.

Black and Yellow version: Blue Moon Fiberarts **Socks That Rock** light weight (superwash merino) in color "*shadow*" (color A), 380 yards, 4.5 oz, 1 skein and Shalimar Yarns **Zoe Sock** (superwash merino) in color "*catalina*" (color B), 450 yards, 3.5 oz, 1 skein.

WPI: 16

Needles: DPNs or circulars in size to give correct gauge (2.75 mm –US size 2 suggested).

Gauge: 8 stitches / 10.5 rows per inch in stockinette knit in round.

Notions: 2 markers, tapestry needle.

Color Suggestions: Contrasting painted, solid or semi-solid colors.

Sizing Notes: Length of foot is measured by trying on sock. This pattern is one size in circumference. To change sizes, increase or decrease needle size and yarn weight to get a different gauge.

Turn heel:

Heel turn is worked only in color B.

Row 1

K19, SSK, K1, turn.

Row 2

Slip first stitch, P6, P2 tog, P1, turn.

Row 3

Slip first stitch, K to 1 stitch before gap formed on previous row, SSK (this will include one stitch on each side of the gap), K1, turn.

Row 4

Slip first stitch, P to 1 stitch before gap formed on previous row, P2 tog (this will include one stitch on each side of the gap), P1, turn.

Repeat Rows 3 and 4 until all side stitches have been worked. You should have 19 stitches on the heel needle. End having completed a WS row.

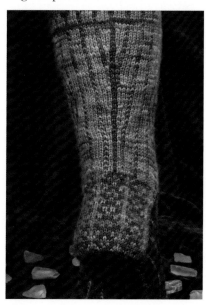

GUSSET

Using heel stitch needle, knit across the heel stitches following Chart 3, starting at stitch 16. Continuing with stitch 35, pick up 15 stitches along the left side of heel flap following Chart 3.

Work across instep stitches following Chart 4.

Pick up another 15 stitches on the other side of the heel flap, following Chart 3 starting at stitch 1.

Work across remaining heel stitches following Chart 3.

You now have 35 instep stitches and 49 heel stitches.

For the Remainder of the Gusset

Instep stitches: Follow Chart 4.

Heel stitches: Follow Chart 3.

When Chart 3 is complete, you now have 35 instep stitches and 31 heel stitches.

FOOT

Continue working both instep and heel stitches in color pattern as established, until foot is the correct length to begin toe shaping (usually this is at the base of the big toe).

TOE

Move one stitch from the beginning and end of instep stitches to heel stitches. You now have 33 instep stitches and 33 heel stitches.

Instep stitches: Follow Chart 5.

Heel stitches: Repeat instep stitches.

When Chart 5 is complete, close toe with Kitchener stitch (p. 124).

Chart 1

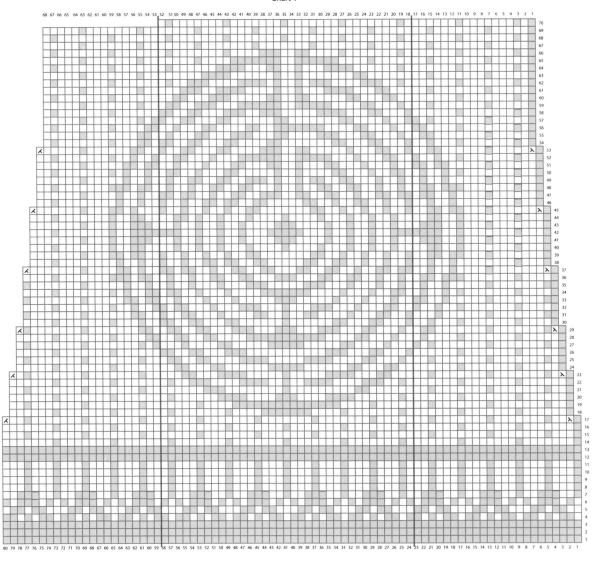

	K in color A
	K in color B
	K2 tog in corresponding color
	SSK in corresponding color

26

Chart 2

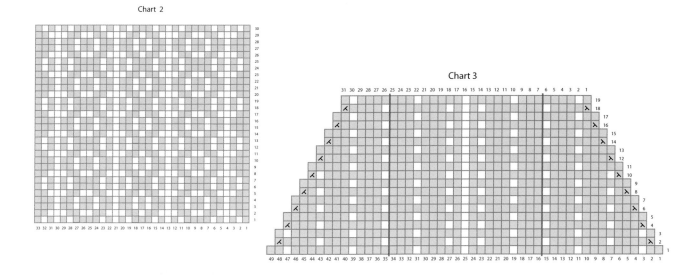

Chart 3

Chart 4

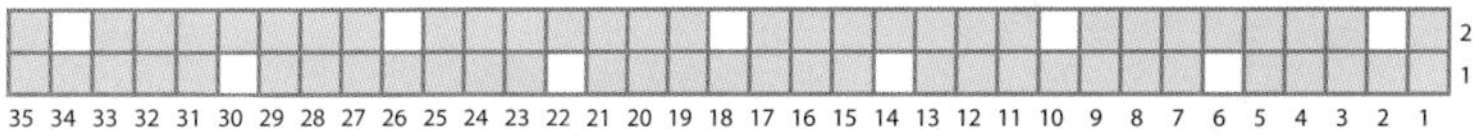

Chart 5

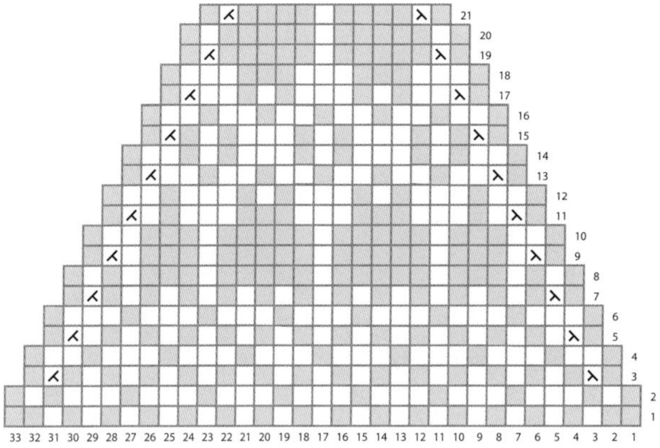

Snow Queen

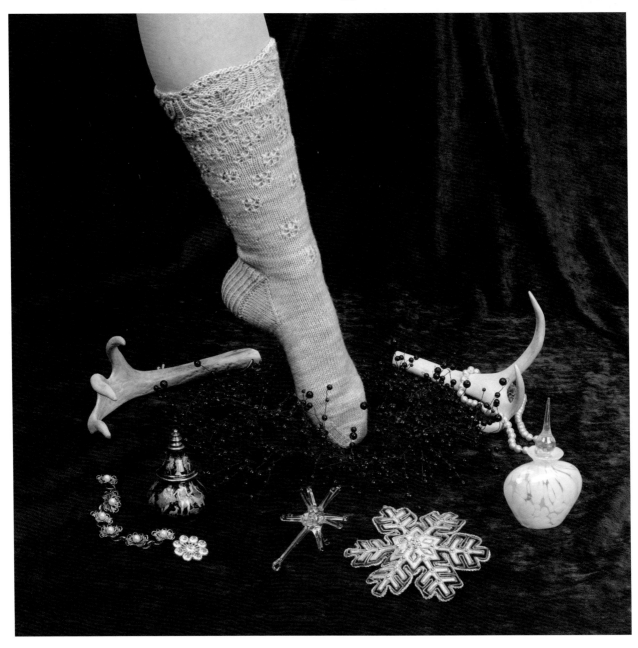

itter cold, snow and ice are the realm of the Snow Queen, where it is always Winter. Luckily we don't have to live in the Snow Queen's land, but just in case you're feeling a bit wintery, these snowy socks with the frosted cuff will keep your toes warm and happy.

Cast On

Cast on 68 stitches and join in the round, taking care not to twist your stitches.

Divide stitches evenly into two groups; instep stitches and heel stitches.

Cuff

K 1 round, P 1 round. Work one round of YO, K2 tog. P 1 round.

Thereafter work following Chart 1. You will have 4 repeats of the chart around the circumference of the sock.

When Chart 1 is complete, continue working following Chart 2. You will have only 1 repeat of the chart around the circumference of the sock. When Chart 2 is completed, begin heel.

You now have 30 instep stitches and 30 heel stitches.

Heel

Heel flap:

Working only the heel stitches, always slipping the first stitch of each row, and working back and forth, work K1 tbl, P1 ribbing for 30 rows or until the heel flap is the correct depth for your heel.

PATTERN NOTES

Finished Circumference Measurements (unstretched):

foot	ankle	mid calf	upper calf
7.25 in	7.25 in	8.0 in	8.25 in

Yarn Used: Blue Moon Fiber Arts **Socks That Rock,** light weight (superwash merino) in color "*winter solstice*", 380 yards, 4.5 oz, 2 skeins.

WPI: 16

Needles: DPNs or circulars in size to give correct gauge (3.25 mm –US size 3 suggested).

Gauge: 8 stitches / 12 rows per inch.

Notions: Tapestry needle.

Color Suggestions: Solid or semi solid colors.

Sizing Notes: Length of foot is measured by trying on sock. This pattern is one size in circumference. To change sizes, increase or decrease needle size and yarn weight to get a different gauge.

Turn heel:

Row 1

K18, SSK, K1, turn.

Row 2

Slip first stitch, P6, P2 tog, P1, turn.

Row 3

Slip first stitch, K to 1 stitch before gap formed on previous row, SSK (this will include one stitch on each side of the gap), K1, turn.

Row 3

Slip first stitch, P to 1 stitch before gap formed on previous row, P2 tog (this will include one stitch on each side of the gap), P1, turn.

Repeat Rows 3 and 4 until all side stitches have been worked. You should have 18 stitches on the heel needle. End having completed a WS row.

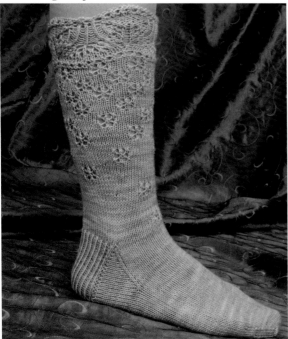

GUSSET

Using heel stitch needle, pick up 16 stitches along side of heel flap. Work across instep, then pick up another 16 stitches on the other side of the flap. You now have 30 instep stitches and 50 heel stitches.

Round 1

Instep stitches: K

Heel stitches: K

Round 2

Instep stitches: K

Heel stitches: K1, SSK, K to last 3 stitches, K2 tog, K1.

Repeat Rounds 1 and 2, decreasing every other row on the heel stitches until you have 30 instep and 30 heel stitches.

FOOT

Instep stitches: K

Heel stitches: K

Repeat until foot is the correct length to begin toe shaping (usually this is at the base of the big toe).

TOE

Round 1

Instep stitches: K

Heel stitches: K

Round 2

Instep stitches: K1, SSK, K to last 3 stitches, K2 tog, K1.

Heel stitches: Repeat instep stitches.

Repeat Rounds 1 and 2 until you have 14 stitches per needle.

Close toe with Kitchener stitch (p. 124).

Chart 2

Chart 1

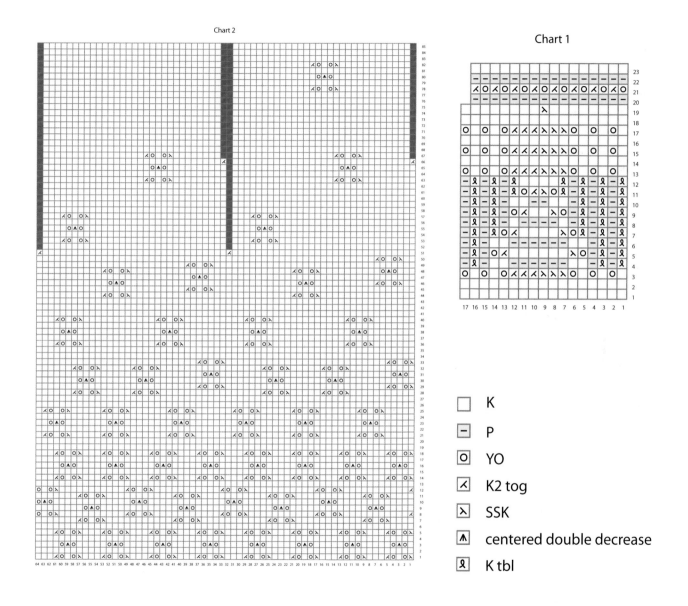

- ☐ K
- − P
- ⊙ YO
- ⟋ K2 tog
- ⟍ SSK
- ⋀ centered double decrease
- ⟑ K tbl

Lothlorien

 he trees in the golden woods of *Lothlorien grace the Elven land in middle earth with a carpet of golden leaves and protection against the ravages of time. These socks contain a little elf magic in the delicate balance between twisting branches and flowery eyelets. Grace your own feet with a bit of elvish lore.*

Cast On

Cast on 24 stitches using the figure 8 cast on (12 loops = 24 stitches), knit one round.

Stitches are divided into two groups, instep stitches and heel stitches. (12 stitches each).

Toe

Round 1

> **Instep stitches:** K
>
> **Heel stitches:** K

Round 2

> **Instep stitches:** K1, M1, K to one stitch before end of instep stitches, M1, K1.
>
> **Heel stitches:** Repeat instep stitches.

Repeat Rounds 1 and 2 until you have 60 stitches total (30 instep stitches, 30 heel stitches).

Foot

Begin Chart 1

For right foot sock

> **Instep stitches:** Follow Chart 1 (right) until complete.
>
> **Heel stitches:** K

For left foot sock: Do the same for the left foot sock, following Chart 1 (left) until complete.

When chart is complete, continue to work each round in stockinette until until until sock measures 5 inches less than total foot length.

Pattern Notes

Finished Circumference Measurements (unstretched):

foot	*ankle*	*mid calf*
7.5 in	7.0 in	9.0 in

Yarn Used: Chameleon Colorworks **Bambino** (bamboo, superwash merino) in color *"moss"*, 400 yards, 3.5 oz, 1 skein.

WPI: 16

Needles: DPNs or circulars in size to give correct gauge (2.75 mm –US size 2 suggested).

Gauge: 8 stitches / 11 rows per inch in stockinette knit in round.

Notions: 2 markers, cable needle, tapestry needle.

Color Suggestions: Solid or semi-solid colors.

Sizing Notes: Length of foot is measured by trying on sock. This pattern is one size in circumference. To change sizes, increase or decrease needle size and yarn weight to get a different gauge.

GUSSET

Place markers

Instep stitches: K

Heel stitches: K1, M1, place Marker 1, K to one stitch before last heel stitch, place Marker 2, M1, K1.

Knit 1 round.

Round 1

Instep stitches: K

Heel stitches: K1, M1, K to marker, slip marker, K to second marker, slip marker, K to 1 stitch before last heel stitch, M1, K1.

Round 2

Instep stitches: K

Heel stitches: K

Repeat rounds 1 and 2 of gusset formation until you have 16 stitches before Marker 1 and after Marker 2.

HEEL

Turn heel

The heel turn is worked only on the heel stitches, excluding the gusset stitches.

Row 1

Work first 16 stitches of heel stitches to Marker 1. Slip marker.

K until 1 stitch is left unworked before Marker 2. Wrap the next stitch. Turn your work.

Row 2

P across until one stitch is left unworked before Marker 1. Wrap the next stitch. Turn your work.

Row 3

K until 1 stitch is left unworked before wrapped stitch. Wrap the next stitch. Turn your work.

Row 4

P until 1 stitch is left unworked before wrapped stitch. Wrap the next stitch. Turn your work.

Repeat Rows 3 and 4 until you have 8 wrapped stitches on either end and 12 live stitches in the middle.

Finish heel turn

Row 1

K all live stitches to the first wrapped stitch. Pick up the stitch and the wrap and knit them together. Pick up the next wrapped stitch and wrap and knit them together. Continue to pick up wrapped stitches and wraps and knit together until you reach the marker. Turn your work.

Row 2

Slip the first stitch. P across to the first wrapped stitch. Pick up wrapped stitch and wrap and purl together. Continue to pick up stitches and wraps and purl together until you reach the marker. Turn your work.

Pick up heel flap

Row 1

Slip first stitch. K to one stitch before last marker. SSK last stitch before marker and first stitch after marker together. You will have to move the marker one stitch to left to avoid trapping the marker. Turn your work.

Row 2

Slip first stitch, P to one stitch before last marker. P last stitch before marker and first stitch after marker together. You will have to move the marker one stitch to left to avoid trapping the marker. Turn your work.

Chart 1 (left)

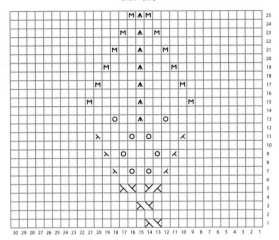

25
24
23
22
21
20
19
18
17
16
15
14
13
12
11
10
9
8
7
6
5
4
3
2
1

30 29 28 27 26 25 24 23 22 21 20 19 18 17 16 15 14 13 12 11 10 9 8 7 6 5 4 3 2 1

Chart 1 (right)

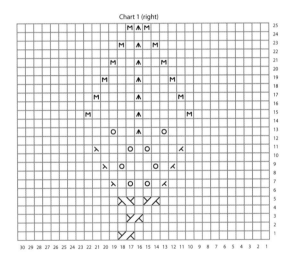

25
24
23
22
21
20
19
18
17
16
15
14
13
12
11
10
9
8
7
6
5
4
3
2
1

30 29 28 27 26 25 24 23 22 21 20 19 18 17 16 15 14 13 12 11 10 9 8 7 6 5 4 3 2 1

☐	K
⋀	centered double decrease
M	M1 lifted
⅄	SSK
⋋	K2 tog
O	YO
⤬	1 over 1 right knit cross
⤬	1 over 1 left knit cross

Repeat Rows 1 and 2 until all gusset stitches have been picked up. You should now have 30 heel and 30 instep stitches.

CUFF

NOTES:

Row 43 *of Chart 2 has a 1 over 1 right cross at each end of the chart. This cable occurs only once per instep and once per heel stitch set, but is shown on either end to indicate that this cable crosses the last instep stitch with the first heel stitch and the last heel stitch with the first instep stitch. In order to accomplish this cross, you will need to move stitches around. Be sure to move the stitches back to their respective groups when cross is complete.*

Begin Chart 2

Follow Chart 2 beginning at bottom right and moving left and upward.

When chart is complete, continue with 6 rounds of K1 tbl, P1 ribbing.

BIND OFF

Bind off using Elizabeth Zimmermann's sewn bind off (p. 123). Weave in ends.

Chart 2

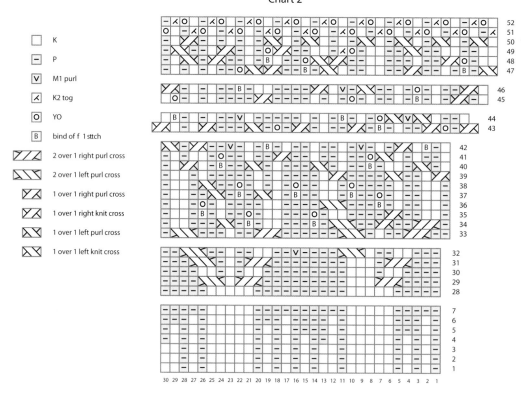

Legend:

□	K
−	P
V	M1 purl
⟋	K2 tog
O	YO
B	bind of f 1 sttch
⟋⟋⟋	2 over 1 right purl cross
⟍⟍⟍	2 over 1 left purl cross
⟋	1 over 1 right purl cross
⟋	1 over 1 right knit cross
⟍	1 over 1 left purl cross
⟍	1 over 1 left knit cross

Pixie

f you are good and kind, you may find a pixie has mended your pots, or swept your hearth, or tended your garden. If you are mean and small, however, you may find a pixie has passed by your house in search of a more deserving human. Here we offer two varieties of pixies, garden pixies and woodland pixies.

SIZE CALCULATIONS:

This sock is constructed sideways so it is important to measure your stitch and row gauge. Use the following worksheet to determine your "foot number" of stitches.

My foot length = _____(A) inches.

Foot length - 2.5 inches = _____(B) inches.

Multiply (B) x 8 st/inch =_____ (C) stitches.

Subtract 12 from (C) = _____ (D). This is your foot number. If your foot number is odd, add or subtract 1 stitch to make it even = _____ (E).

Cast on number = (E) + 52= _____ (F).

The charts for this pattern have red vertical lines denoting the spot where the markers are. Some sections of the chart have a variable number of stitches depending on what your "foot number" is. These sections have only a small representative number of stitches as a place holder.

CAST ON

With waste yarn, provisionally cast on (p. 115) (F) number of stitches from the worksheet above. (for women's size 7 we used 40 stitches (E) + 62 = 102 total).

PATTERN NOTES

Finished Circumference Measurements (unstretched):

foot	ankle
8 in	8 in

Yarn Used: Pagewood farms **Chugiak Sock** (superwash merino) in colors "*camo*"(color A) and "*watermelon*" (pink) (color B) or "*harvest*" (brown) (alternate color B), 450 yards, 4 oz, 1 skein each.

WPI: 19

Needles: Straight or circulars in size to give correct gauge (2.75 mm –US size 2 suggested).

Gauge: 8 stitches / 12 rows per inch in garter stitch.

Notions: 3 different markers, tapestry needle, size E crochet hook.

Color Suggestions: Solid, semi solid or painted yarns.

Sizing Notes: This sock is calculated by you to fit your foot. To increase circumference add more green rows between pink (or brown) pattern rows.

PLACE MARKERS

Set up rows

In waste yarn, K 1 row, placing markers as follows: K12, place Marker 1, K foot number of stitches (D), place Marker 2, K1, place Marker 3. Purl back with waste yarn.

INSTEP

Follow Chart 1 for 48 rows (2 repeats of Chart 1 including short rows).

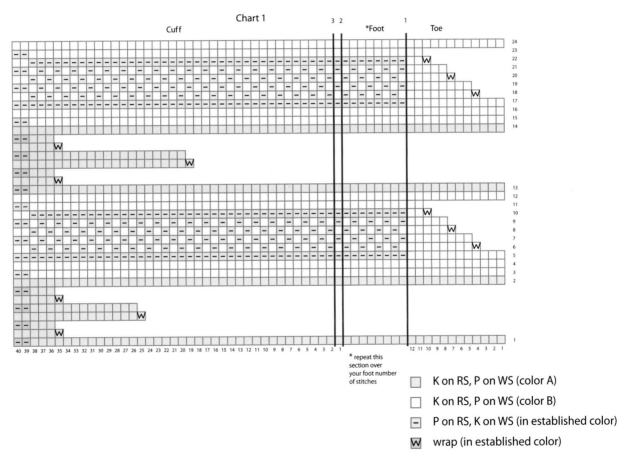

Chart 1

Cuff   3 2   *Foot   1   Toe

* repeat this section over your foot number of stitches

☐ K on RS, P on WS (color A)

☐ K on RS, P on WS (color B)

□ P on RS, K on WS (in established color)

W wrap (in established color)

39

HEEL

Rows 1-16

> **Beginning of row - Marker 2:** Follow Chart 2.

> **Marker 2 - Marker 3:** Follow Chart 3.

> **Marker 3 - End of row:** Follow Chart 2.

You now have 31 stitches between Markers 2 and 3.

Rows 17-31

When Chart 3 is complete, follow Chart 2 on all stitches for 15 rows. Stitches between Markers 2 and 3 are knit in stockinette.

Rows 32-47

> **Beginning of row - Marker 2:** Follow Chart 2.

> **Marker 2 - Marker 3:** Follow Chart 4.

> **Marker 3 - End of row:** Follow Chart 2.

You now have 1 stitch between Markers 2 and 3.

Row 48:

Graft sides together in color A using Kitchener stitch (p. 124).

FINISHING

Sew toe together. Weave in ends.

Crochet Edging

Round 1

Using color B yarn, make a slip knot loop on your crochet hook and attach to the top edge using a slip stitch. Chain 3, slip stitch into the second stitch from your previous slip stitch. Repeat all the way around the circumference, ending with a slip stitch in your original spot.

Round 2

Chain 1. Work 3 DC's and one SC into the chain 3 loop. In next loop work 1 SC, 3 DC, 1 SC into the chain loop. Continue in this manner all the way around the circumference. Slip stitch into your original Chain 1 stitch. Break yarn and pull through last loop.

Chart 2

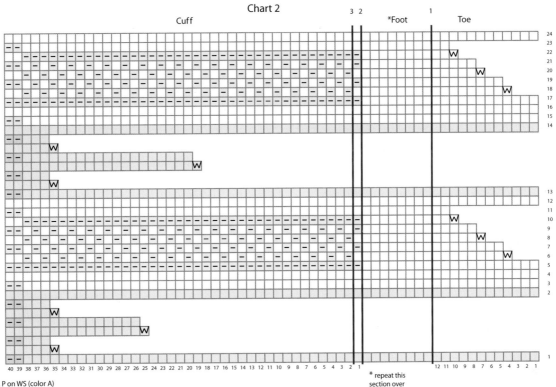

Cuff   3 2   *Foot   1   Toe

- ☐ K on RS, P on WS (color A)
- ☐ K on RS, P on WS (color B)
- ⊟ P on RS, K on WS (in established color)
- Ⓦ wrap (in established color)

* repeat this section over your foot number of stitches

Chart 3

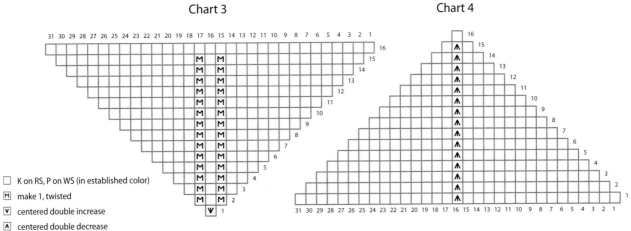

- ☐ K on RS, P on WS (in established color)
- Ⓜ make 1, twisted
- Ⓥ centered double increase
- Ⓐ centered double decrease

Chart 4

41

La Licorne

a dame a la licorne, a series of medieval tapestries, depicts a lady and a unicorn in a field of red surrounded by flowers. A banner at the top of the final tapestry reads "a mon seul desir", to my only desire. It is a mystery what is happening in the picture. Has the lady tamed the unicorn? These charming socks have a banner at the top proclaiming "a mon seul desir" and flowers on a field of red. Peeking out from the heel is a rabbit, perhaps he knows the answer to the mystery?

Cast On

Cast on 72 stitches in color A and join in the round, taking care not to twist your stitches.

Divide stitches into two groups; instep stitches (32 stitches) and heel stitches (40 stitches).

Cuff

Ribbing:

Work 6 rounds of K2 tbl, P2 ribbing in color A (red).

Set up round:

K one round increasing evenly by 6 stitches. You now have 78 stitches, arrange to give 32 instep stitches and 46 heel stitches.

Begin Chart 1

Work following Chart 1.

When Chart 1 is completed, continue knitting in stockinette, decreasing by 2 stitches in the center of the heel stitches every 5th row until you have 64 stitches, 32 instep stitches and 32 heel stitches.

Heel

Heel flap:

Working only the heel stitches, always slipping the first stitch of each row, and working back and forth, knit in stockinette for 30 rows.

Pattern Notes

Finished Circumference Measurements (unstretched):

foot	ankle	mid calf
8.0 in	8.0 in	9.0 in

Yarn Used: Dye Dreams **Luster Sox** (bluefaced leicester wool) in colors *"brick"* (color A) *"medium denim"* (color B) and *"gold"* (color C), 415 yards, 3.5 oz, 1 skein of red, 50 yards each of blue and gold. A variety of small pieces of sock yarn for embroidery.

WPI: 17

Needles: DPNs or circulars in size to give correct gauge (2.75 mm –US size 2 suggested).

Gauge: 8 stitches / 12 rows per inch.

Notions: Markers, tapestry needle.

Color Suggestions: Solids, semi solids in "medieval" colors.

Sizing Notes: This sock is given in one size, but is easily adjustable. To increase circumference, add more stitches and increase spacing between words in lettering chart.

Turn heel:

Row 1

K18, SSK, K1, turn.

Row 2

Slip first stitch, P5, P2 tog, P1, turn.

Row 3

Slip first stitch, K to 1 stitch before gap formed on previous row, SSK (this will include one stitch on each side of the gap), K1, turn.

Row 4

Slip first stitch, P to 1 stitch before gap formed on previous row, P2 tog (this will include one stitch on each side of the gap), P1, turn.

Repeat Rows 3 and 4 until all side stitches have been worked. You should have 18 stitches on the heel needle. End having completed a WS row.

GUSSET

Using heel stitch needle, pick up 16 stitches along side of heel flap.

Work across instep stitches in stockinette.

Pick up another 16 stitches on the other side of the heel flap.

You now have 32 instep stitches and 50 heel stitches.

Round 1

Instep stitches: K

Heel stitches: K1, SSK, K to last 3 heel stitches, K2 tog, K1.

Round 2

Instep stitches: K

Heel stitches: K

Repeat Rounds 1 and 2, decreasing every other round on the heel stitches until you have 32 instep stitches and 32 heel stitches.

FOOT

Continue working in stockinette until foot is the correct length to begin toe shaping (usually this is at the base of the big toe).

Chart 1

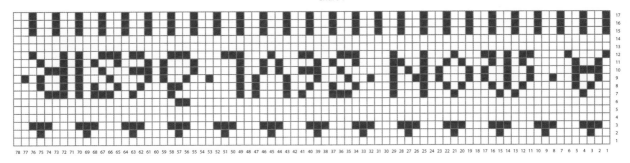

☐ color B
■ color C

TOE

Round 1

    Instep stitches: K

    Heel stitches: K

Round 2

    Instep stitches: K1, SSK, K to last 3 stitches, K2 tog, K1.

    Heel stitches: Repeat instep stitches.

Repeat Rounds 1 and 2 until you have 14 stitches per needle.

Close toe with Kitchener stitch (p. 124).

FINISHING

Embroider flowers randomly on cuff of both socks using laisy daisy and stem stitch in a variety of colors. Duplicate stitch rabbit from Chart 2 on one heel using white yarn.

Chart 2

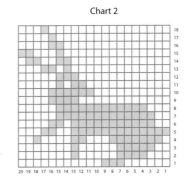

45

Naiad

pirits of fresh waters, Naiads preside over streams and springs. Propose to a Naiad and she will extract a promise. If you are faithful to your promise she will love you forever. These socks evoke the swirling currents of rivers and promise to delight your toes with their unusual construction and exceptional fit.

SIZE CALCULATIONS

This sock is constructed sideways so it is important to measure your stitch and row gauge. Use the following worksheet to determine your "foot number" of stitches.

My foot length = _____(A) inches.

Foot length - 2.5 inches = _____(B) inches.

Multiply (B) x 8 st/inch =_____ (C) stitches.

Subtract 12 from (C) = _____ (D). This is your foot number. Add stitches to (or subtract from) (D) until it is a multiple of 9 = _____(E)

Cast on number = (E) + 58= _____ (F).

The charts for this pattern have red vertical lines denoting the spot where the markers are. Some sections of the chart have a variable number of stitches depending on what your "foot number" is. These sections have only a small representative number of stitches as a place holder.

CAST ON

With waste yarn, provisionally cast on (p. 115) (F) number of stitches from the worksheet above (for women's size 7 we used 45 stitches (E) + 59 = 103 total).

PATTERN NOTES

Finished Circumference Measurements (unstretched):

foot	ankle
8.5 inches	8.5 inches

Yarn Used: Shalimar Yarns **Zoe Sock** (superwash merino) in color *"cornucopia"*, 450 yards, 3.5 oz, 1 skein.

WPI: 16

Needles: Straights or circulars in size to give correct gauge (2.75 mm –US size 2 suggested).

Gauge: 8 stitches / 11 rows per inch in stockinette knit flat.

Notions: 4 different markers, tapestry needle.

Color Suggestions: Painted, solid or semi-solid colors.

Sizing Notes: This sock is calculated by you to fit your foot. To increase circumference add more pattern rows before heel increase and before heel decrease.

PLACE MARKERS

Set up rows

In waste yarn, K 1 row, placing markers as follows:

K12, place Marker 1, K foot number of stitches (D), place Marker 2, K1, place Marker 3, K until 10 stitches remain, place marker 4. K to end. Purl back in waste yarn.

INSTEP

Begin Instep:

Follow Chart 1 for 48 rows (3 repeats of Chart 1).

HEEL

Rows 1-16

Beginning of row - Marker 2: Follow Chart 2.
Marker 2 - Marker 3: Follow Chart 3.
Marker 3 - End of row: Follow Chart 2.

You now have 31 stitches between Markers 2 and 3.

Rows 17-31:

When Chart 3 is complete, follow Chart 2 on all stitches for 15 rows. Stitches between Markers 2 and 3 are worked in stockinette.

Rows 32-47:

Beginning of row - Marker 2: Follow Chart 2.

Marker 2 - Marker 3: Follow Chart 4.

Marker 3 - End of row: Follow Chart 2.

You now have 1 stitch between Markers 2 and 3.

Graft sides together using Kitchener stitch in pattern (p. 124).

FINISHING

Sew toe together. Weave in ends.

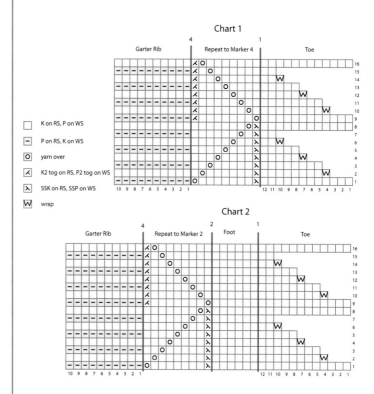

Chart 1

Chart 2

☐ K on RS, P on WS
— P on RS, K on WS
○ yarn over
⊼ K2 tog on RS, P2 tog on WS
⊼ SSK on RS, SSP on WS
W wrap

Chart 3 Chart 4

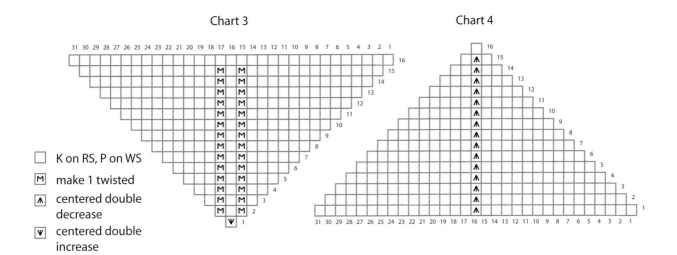

- ☐ K on RS, P on WS
- Ⓜ make 1 twisted
- Ⓐ centered double decrease
- Ⓥ centered double increase

Tristan & Isolde

*wo star-crossed lovers ensnared in a triangle, Tristan and Isolde were bound together by a love potion gone wrong. These cable crossed socks require no potions to make you love them. They are sturdy, warm and look good in every color, and are equally handsome for both men and women.*

Cast On

Cast on 24 stitches using the figure 8 cast on (12 loops = 24 stitches), knit one round.

Stitches are divided into two groups, instep stitches and heel stitches. (12 stitches each).

Toe

Round 1

   Instep stitches: K

   Heel stitches: K

Round 2

   Instep stitches: K1, M1, K to one stitch before end of instep stitches, M1, K1.

   Heel stitches: Repeat instep stitches.

Repeat Rounds 1 and 2 until you have 66 (68, 72) stitches total. Arrange stitches into two groups; 34 (34, 36) instep stitches, 32 (34, 36) heel stitches.

Foot

Begin Chart 1

   Instep stitches: K7 (7, 8), follow Chart 1, K7 (7, 8). This will center the chart in the instep stitches.

   Heel stitches: K

Continue working foot, repeating Chart 1 as necessary, until until sock measures 5.5 inches less than total foot length.

Pattern Notes

Finished Circumference Measurements (un-stretched):

	foot	*ankle*	*mid calf*
small	7.75 in	7.75 in	9.5 in
medium	8.0 in	8.0 in	9.8 in
large	8.5 in	8.5 in	10.25 in

Yarn Used: Dye Dreams **Comfy Sox** (superwash merino) in color "*charcoal*", 490 yds, 3.5 oz, 1 skein.

WPI: 17

Needles: DPNs or circulars in size to give correct gauge (2.75 mm –US size 2 suggested).

Gauge: 8 stitches / 11 rows per inch in stockinette knit in round.

Notions: 3 markers, cable needle, tapestry needle.

Color Suggestions: solid or semi solid, subtle painted colors.

Sizing Notes: Length of foot is measured by trying on sock. This pattern has 3 sizes in circumference, you may also change sizes by changing needle and yarn size.

Chart 1

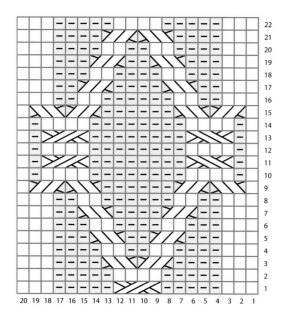

Chart 2

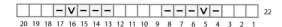

GUSSET

Place markers

Instep stitches: Continue following Chart 1 as established.

Heel stitches: K1, M1, place Marker 1, K to one stitch before last heel stitch, place Marker 2, M1, K1.

Round 1

Instep stitches: Continue following Chart 1 as established.

Heel stitches: K1, M1, K to marker, slip marker, K to second marker, slip marker, K to 1 stitch before last heel stitch, M1, K1.

Round 2

Instep stitches: Continue following Chart 1 as established.

Heel stitches: K

Repeat Rounds 1 and 2 of gusset formation until you have 16 stitches before Marker 1 and after Marker 2.

HEEL

Turn heel

The heel turn is worked only on the heel stitches, excluding the gusset stitches.

Row 1

Work first 16 st of heel stitches to Marker 1. Slip marker.

K until 1 stitch is left unworked before Marker 2. Wrap the next stitch. Turn your work.

Row 2

P across until one stitch is left unworked before Marker 1. Wrap the next stitch. Turn your work.

Row 3

K until 1 stitch is left unworked before wrapped stitch. Wrap the next stitch. Turn your work.

Row 4

P until 1 stitch is left unworked before wrapped stitch. Wrap the next stitch. Turn your work.

Repeat Rows 3 and 4 until you have 8 wrapped stitches on either end and 14 (16, 18) live stitches in the middle.

Finish heel turn

Row 1

K all live stitches to the first wrapped stitch. Pick up the stitch and the wrap and knit them together. Pick up the next wrapped stitch and wrap and knit them together. Continue to pick up wrapped stitches and wraps and knit together until you reach the marker. Turn your work.

Row 2

Slip the first stitch. P across to the first wrapped stitch. Pick up wrapped stitch and wrap and purl together. Continue to pick up stitches and wraps and purl together until you reach the marker. Turn your work.

Pick up heel flap

Row 1

Slip first stitch. K to one stitch before last marker. SSK last stitch before marker and first stitch after marker together. You will have to move the marker one stitch to the left to avoid trapping the marker. Turn your work.

Row 2:

Slip first stitch, P to one stitch before last marker. P last stitch before marker and first stitch after marker together. You will have to move the marker one stitch to the left to avoid trapping the marker. Turn your work.

Repeat rows 1 and 2 until all gusset stitches have been picked up. You should now have 34 (34, 36) instep stitches, 32 (34, 36) heel stiches).

CUFF

Place markers.

Beginning with instep stitches, K7 (7, 8) then pick up Chart 1 at the row where you left off and work across Chart 1, K2 (med: K2, M1 lifted, large: K4), work Chart 1, K2, (3, 4) work Chart 1 (chart will wrap around to instep stitches). There are 3 repeats of the chart around the cuff with 2 (3, 4) stitches between repeats.

Begin Chart 2

Continue following Chart 1 until you reach Row 21, at this point work Chart 2 instead of the last row of Chart 1.

Begin Chart 3

Follow Chart 3 until chart is complete.

Begin Chart 4

Follow Chart 4 until chart is complete.

Alternate ribbing (pink "*Isolde*" sock) - substitute the following for rows 32-38 of Chart 4:

K one round, P one round, K 1 round.

Work 6 rounds K1 tbl, P1 ribbing.

K one round, P one round, K 1 round.

BIND OFF

Use Elizabeth Zimmermann's sewn bind off (p. 123).

Weave in ends.

	K
−	P
■	no stitch
ℛ	K tbl
⋋	P2 tog
⋁	M1 purl
⟋⟋	2 over 1 right purl cable cross
⟍⟍	2 over 1 left purl cable cross
⟋⟋	2 over 2 right knit cable cross
⟍⟍	2 over 2 left knit cable cross

Chart 3

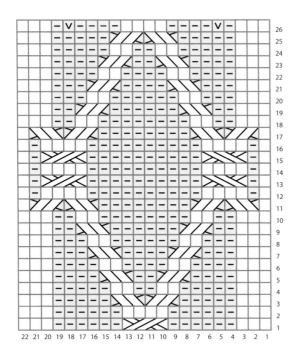

Chart 4

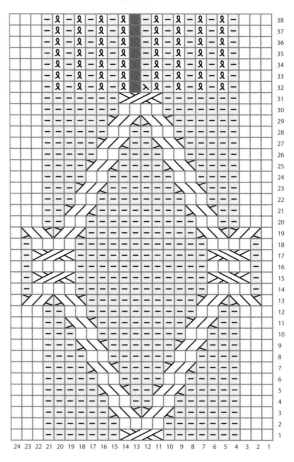

Mirror Mirror

 mirror never lies, it reflects whatever is before it. A mirror, however, does show you opposites. These mirrored socks are mirrored twice; once within the sock and once on the feet. They will delight you with their beauty and symmetry.

Cast On

Cast on 96 stitches and join in the round, taking care not to twist your stitches.

Cuff

Ribbing:

Work 6 rounds of K2 tbl, P2 ribbing in color A.

Set up round:

K 1 round increasing evenly by 6 stitches. You now have 102 stitches.

Begin Chart 1

Work following Chart 1.

When Chart 1 is completed, begin heel. You should have 64 stitches.

Heel

Set up round:

Rearrange stitches to make 2 sets of stitches, instep stitches and heel stitches. Stitches 1-16 are heel stitches. Stitches 17-48 are instep stitches. Stitches 49-64 are heel stitches.

Heel flap:

Working only the heel stitches, always slipping the first stitch of each row, and working back and forth, follow Chart 2. When Chart 2 is completed, turn heel.

Pattern Notes

Finished Circumference Measurements (unstretched):

foot	ankle	mid calf	upper calf
8.0 in	8.0 in	11.0 in	12.75

Yarn Used: Dye Dreams **Luster Sox** (superwash BFL) in colors "*moss*" (color A) and "*peacock*" (color B), 415 yards, 3.5 oz, 2 skeins each.

WPI: 17

Needles: DPNs or circulars in size to give correct gauge (2.75 mm –US size 2 suggested).

Gauge: 8 stitches / 11 rows per inch in stockinette knit in round.

Notions: Tapestry needle.

Color Suggestions: Painted or solid colors with good contrast between the two colors used.

Sizing Notes: Length of foot is measured by trying on sock. This pattern is one size in circumference. To change sizes, increase or decrease needle size and yarn weight to get a different gauge. Because colorwork has little elasticity, unstretched circumferences are larger.

Turn heel:

Heel turn is worked only in color A.

Row 1

K18, SSK, K1, turn.

Row 2

Slip first stitch, P5, P2 tog, P1, turn.

Row 3

Slip first stitch, K to 1 stitch before gap formed on previous row, SSK (this will include one stitch on each side of the gap), K1, turn.

Row 4

Slip first stitch, P to 1 stitch before gap formed on previous row, P2 tog (this will include one stitch on each side of the gap), P1, turn.

Repeat Rows 3 and 4 until all side stitches have been worked. You should have 18 stitches on the heel needle. End having completed a WS row.

Gusset

Round 1

Work across heel stitches following Chart 3 beginning at stitch 17 and ending with stitch 34. Using heel stitch needle, pick up 16 stitches along side of heel flap following Chart 3, beginning at stitch 35 and ending with stitch 50.

Work across instep stitches following Chart 3 beginning at stitch 10 and ending at stitch 41.

Pick up another 16 stitches on the other side of the heel flap beginning with stitch 1 and ending with stitch 16 of Chart 3.

You now have 32 instep stitches and 50 heel stitches.

Round 2

Instep stitches: Continue in colors as established.

Heel stitches: Follow Chart 3.

Repeat Round 2 until Chart 3 is finished. You should have 32 instep stitches and 32 heel stitches.

Foot

Continue working in color pattern as established until foot is the correct length to begin toe shaping (usually this is at the base of the big toe).

Toe

Round 1

Instep stitches: Work in color pattern as established.

Heel stitches: Work in color pattern as established.

Round 2

Instep stitches: Working in color pattern as established, K1, SSK, K to last 3 stitches, K2 tog, K1.

Heel stitches: Repeat instep stitches.

Repeat Rounds 1 and 2 until you have 14 stitches per needle.

Close toe with Kitchener stitch (p. 124), weave in ends.

Reverse colors for second sock.

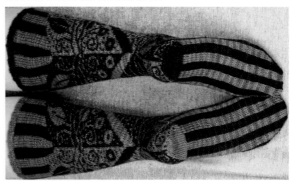

Chart 1

color A
color B

reverse colors on second sock

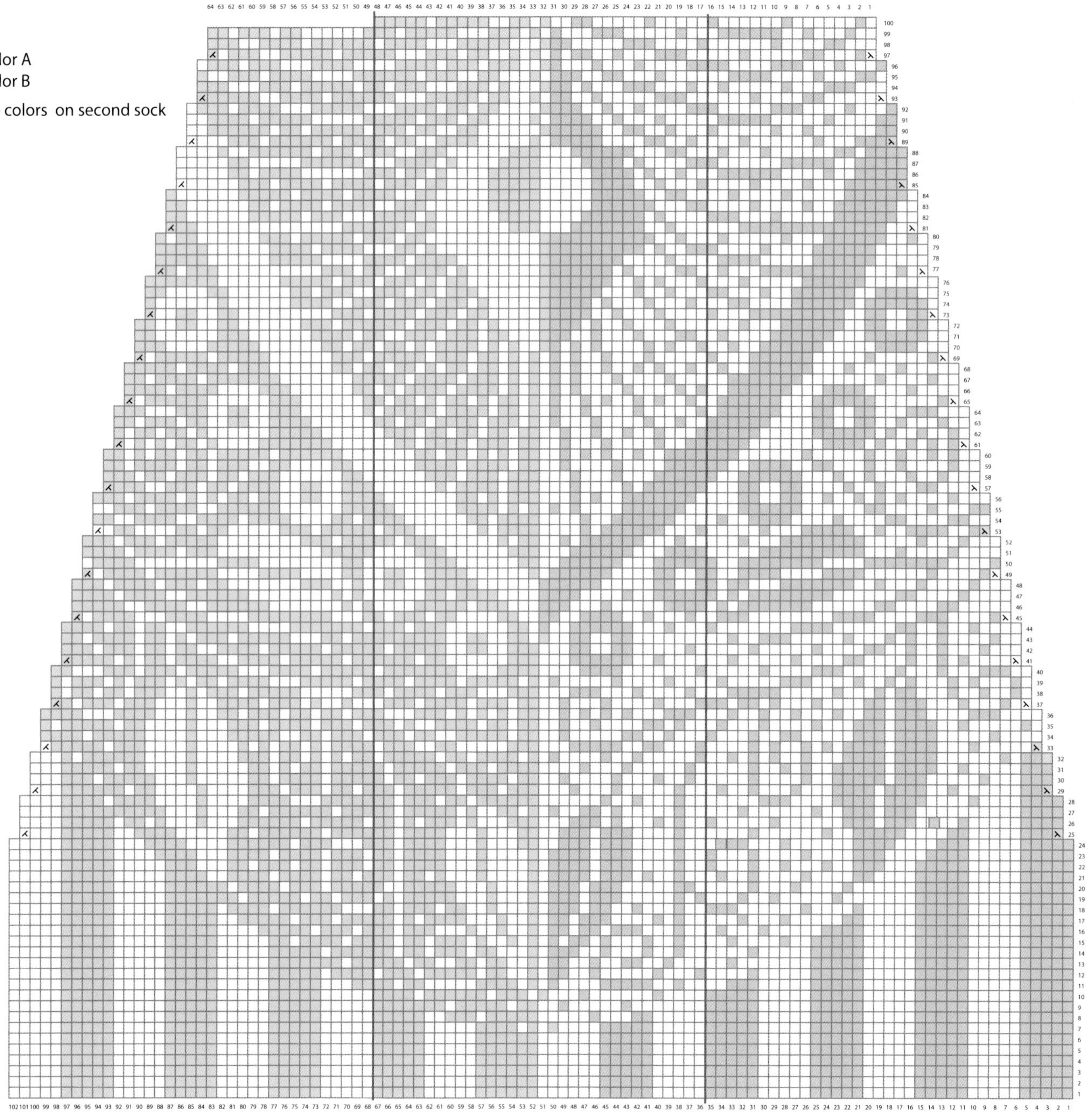

Chart 2

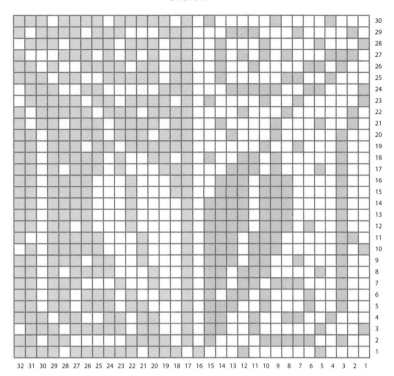

- ☐ (gray) K in color A
- ☐ K in color B
- ⊼ K2 tog in corresponding color
- ⊻ SSK in corresponding color

Chart 3

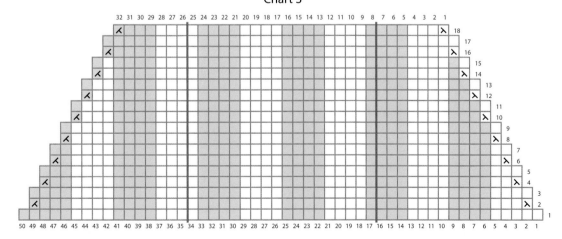

Selkie

 enizens of the deep, Selkies are shapeshifting seal-humans. Steal a Selkie's seal skin and you make her bound to the land. Although Selkies may come ashore from time to time and change into human form, they always long for the sea. These socks are for sea loving creatures of all types. Long strands of seaweed run from toe to top, reminding us of the primordial ocean and all her glories. Make some silky Selkie socks to wear when the lure of the sea pulls at your soul.

Cast On

Cast on 78 (80, 84) stitches and join in the round, taking care not to twist your stitches.

Divide stitches evenly into two groups; instep stitches and heel stitches.

Cuff

Work 8 rounds of K1 tbl, P1 ribbing.

Place markers.

Starting with instep stitches;

Small: P26, place marker. Repeat 2 more times (3 total).

Medium: P1, make 1 purl (purl into front and back of stitch), P24, place marker. *P27, place marker, Repeat from * 1 more time (3 total).

Large: P28, place marker. Repeat 2 more times (3 total).

You now have 39 (40, 42) instep stitches and 39 (41, 42) heel stitches.

Begin Chart 1

Work following Chart 1. You will have 3 repeats of the chart around the circumference of the sock.

When Chart 1 is complete, continue working following Chart 2. You will have 3 repeats of the chart around the circumference of the sock.

Pattern Notes

Finished Circumference Measurements (unstretched):

	foot	ankle	mid calf
small	7.5 in	7.5 in	7.5 in
medium	7.9 in	7.9 in	7.9 in
large	8.25 in	8.25 in	8.25 in

Yarn Used: Curious Creek **Wasonga** (superwash merino) in color "*good witch*," 493 yards, 3.5 oz, 1 skein.

WPI: 16

Needles: DPNs or circulars in size to give correct gauge (2.75 mm –US size 2 suggested).

Gauge: 8 stitches / 11 rows per inch in stockinette knit in round.

Notions: 3 markers, tapestry needle.

Color Suggestions: Painted, solid / semi-solid colors.

Sizing Notes: Length of foot is measured by trying on sock. This pattern has 3 sizes in circumference, you may also change sizes by changing needle and yarn size.

When Chart 2 is completed, you will have 30 (31, 33) instep stitches and 30 (32, 33) heel stitches.

For right foot sock: Continue on to heel.

For left foot sock: Rearrange stitches in the following manner: Move the last 13 (14, 16) stitches from the heel stitches to the beginning of the instep stitches, and move the last 13 (14, 16) instep stitches to the beginning of the heel stitches. Continue on to the heel.

HEEL

Heel flap:

Working only the heel stitches, always slipping the first stitch of each row, and working back and forth, work K1 tbl, P1 ribbing for 30 rows or until the heel flap is the correct depth for your heel.

Turn heel:

Row 1

P18 (18, 19), P2 tog, P1, turn.

Row 2

Slip first stitch, K 6 (4, 5), SSK, K1, turn.

Row 3

Slip first stitch, P to 1 stitch before gap formed on previous row, P2 tog (this will include one stitch on each side of the gap), P1, turn.

Row 4

Slip first stitch, K to 1 stitch before gap formed on previous row, SSK (this will include one stitch on each side of the gap), K1, turn.

Repeat Rows 3 and 4 until all side stitches have been worked. You should have 18 (18, 19) stitches on the heel needle. End having completed a WS row.

GUSSET

P across heel stitches. Using heel stitch needle, pick up 16 stitches along side of heel flap. Work across instep, then pick up another 16 stitches on the other side of the flap. You now have 30 (31, 33) instep stitches and 50 (50, 51) heel stitches.

Note: The following directions are for the right foot sock. For the left foot sock instep stitches, P13 (14, 16), then work Chart 3.

Round 1

  Instep stitches: Follow Chart 3, P13 (14, 16).

  Heel stitches: P14, place Marker 1,

  P 22 (22, 23), place Marker 2, P14.

Round 2

  Instep stitches: Continue following Chart 3, P13 (14, 16).

  Heel stitches: P14, slip marker, P2 tog, P to last 2 stitches before Marker 2, SSP, slip marker, P14.

Repeat Rounds 1 and 2, decreasing every other row on the heel stitches until you have 30 (31, 33) instep stitches and 30 (32, 33) heel stitches.

Chart 1

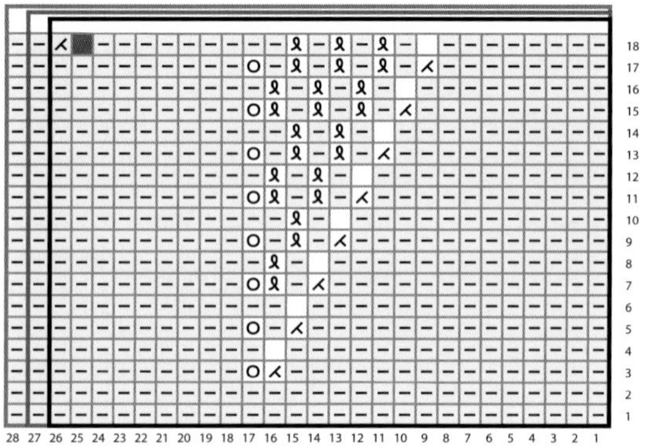

FOOT

Instep stitches: Continue following Chart 3.

Heel stitches: P

Repeat until foot is the correct length to begin toe shaping (usually this is at the base of the big toe).

TOE

Round 1

Instep stitches: P

Heel stitches: P

Round 2

Instep stitches: P1, P2 tog, P to last 3 stitches, SSP, P1.

Heel stitches: Repeat instep stitches.

Small and Large sizes: Repeat Rounds 1 and 2 until you have 14 instep and 14 heel stitches.

Medium size. Repeat Rounds 1 and 2 until you have 15 instep stitches and 16 heel stitches.

Instep stitches: P

Heel stitches: P7, P2 tog, P7.

FINISHING

Close toe with Kitchener stitch (p. 124).

■	no stitch
□	K
−	P
O	YO
ℓ	K tbl
⟋	K2 tog
⟍	SSK
⟋	P2 tog

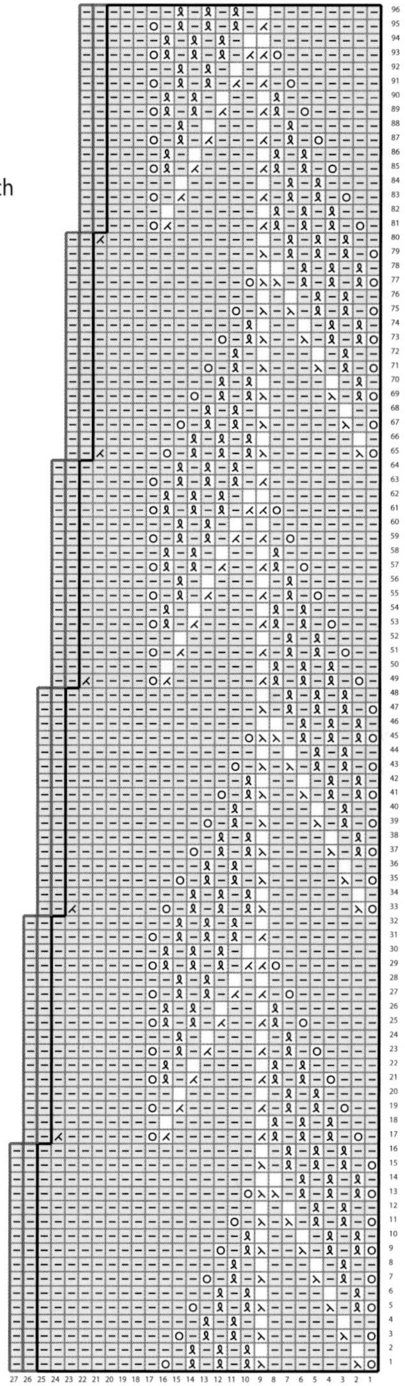

Chart 3

Chart 2

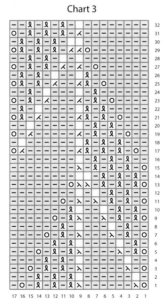

Changeling

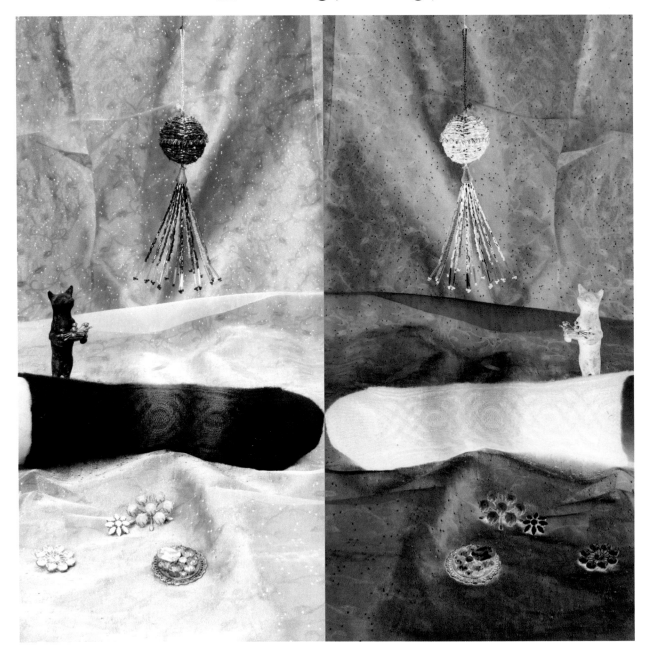

 *imicing their human counterparts, changelings come to us from other realms to partake of the richness and joy of human life, intertwining effortlessly in human society. These socks have cables that intertwine gracefully up the front and back of the sock, and feature a yarn that changes colors effortlessly.*

Cast On

Cast on 24 stitches using the figure 8 cast on (12 loops = 24 stitches), knit one round.

Stitches are divided into two groups, instep stitches and heel stitches. (12 stitches each).

Toe

Round 1

> **Instep stitches:** K

> **Heel stitches:** K

Round 2

> **Instep stitches:** K1, M1, K to one stitch before end of instep stitches, M1, K1.

> **Heel stitches:** Repeat instep stitches.

Repeat Rounds 1 and 2 until you have 70 (74, 78) stitches total.

Foot

Rearrange stitches so that you have 38 instep stitches and 32 (36, 40) heel stitches.

Begin Chart 1

> **Instep stitches:** Follow Chart 1, Rows 1-31 only. Repeat complete chart by following Row 31 with Row 1 again.

> **Heel stitches:** K

Continue to work in this manner until until until sock measures 2.75 inches less than total foot length.

Pattern Notes

Finished Circumference Measurements (unstretched):

	foot	ankle	mid calf
small	7.5 in	7.0 in	8.5 in
medium	8.0 in	8.0 in	8.9 in
large	8.5 in	8.5 in	9.4 in

Yarn Used: Schoppel Wolle **Zauberball** (wool/nylon) color *"brombeeren"*, 3.5 oz, 400 yards, 1 skein.

WPI: 18

Needles: DPNs or circulars in size to give correct gauge (2.5 mm –US size 1 suggested).

Gauge: 10 stitches / 13 rows per inch in stockinette knit in round.

Notions: Cable needle, tapestry needle.

Color Suggestions: Painted, solid or semi-solid colors.

Sizing Notes: Length of foot is measured by trying on sock. This pattern has 3 sizes in circumference; you may also change sizes by changing needle and yarn size.

Heel Flap

Work the first 8 (9, 10) heel stitches, place marker. These 8 (9, 10) heel stitches are called "side heel stitches." K the next 16 (18, 20) heel stitches. Turn work, leaving 8 (9, 10) side heel stitches on the other side. Slip first stitch, P across to marker. Turn work. Continue working back and forth across the center 16 (18, 20) stitches in stockinette, always slipping the first stitch, for 30 rows. End having completed a WS row.

Heel Turn

Turn heel

The heel turn is worked only on the center 16 (18, 20) heel stitches.

Row 1

K10 (10, 12), SSK, K1, turn

Row 2

Slip first stitch, P5 (3, 5), P2 tog, P1, turn.

Row 3

Slip first stitch, K to 1 stitch before gap formed on previous row, SSK (this will include one stitch on each side of the gap), K1, turn.

Row 4

Slip first stitch, P to 1 stitch before gap formed on previous row, P2 tog (this will include one stitch on each side of the gap), P1, turn.

Repeat Rows 3 and 4 until all side stitches have been worked. You should have 10 (10, 12) center heel stitches. End having completed a WS row.

Gusset

K across the remaining heel stitches. Using heel stitch needle, pick up 16 stitches along side of heel flap, one in each slipped stitch plus one gap stitch. Add the 8 (9, 10) side heel stitches to the heel needle. Work across instep stitches following Chart 1. Add the other 8 (9, 10) side heel stitches, pick up 16 stitches along flap, one in each slipped stitch plus one gap stitch, K to end of heel stitches. You now have 58 (60, 64) heel stitches.

Notes:

For small size: *Use the stitches within the black frame on Chart 2 for the heel stitches.*

For medium size: *Use the stitches within the red frame on Chart 2 for the heel stitches.*

For large size: *Use the stitches within the blue frame on Chart 2 for the heel stitches.*

Round 1

Instep stitches: Continue following Chart 1.

Heel stitches: Follow Chart 2, starting at the same row being used on Chart 1 and centering chart in the heel stitches. Excess heel stitches flanking Chart 2 are worked in stockinette.

Round 2

Instep stitches: Work following Chart 1.

Heel stitches: SSK, work following Chart 2 to last 2 stitches, K2 tog.

Repeat Rounds 1 and 2 decreasing every other row on the heel stitches until you have 38 instep stitches and 32 (36, 40) heel stitches.

CUFF

Instep stitches: Continue to follow Chart 1, picking up where you left off.

Heel stitches: Starting at the same row as you are at on Chart 1, follow Chart 2.

When Row 31 is complete, continue on to Row 93 of Charts 1 and 2. When Charts 1 and 2 are complete, repeat Row 93 six more times, then bind off.

BIND OFF

Use Elizabeth Zimmermann's sewn bind off (p. 123).

☐ K

⊟ P

⊠ K tbl

⊻ M1 purl

⬚ 2 over 1 right purl cross

⬚ 2 over 1 left purl cross

⬚ 2 over 2 right knit cross

⬚ 2 over 2 left knit cross

⬚ 2 over 2 right purl cross

⬚ 2 over 2 left purl cross

Chart 1

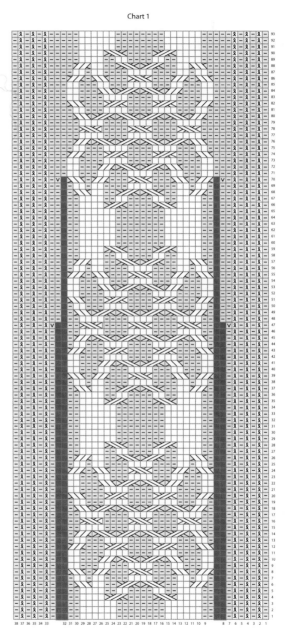

Chart 2

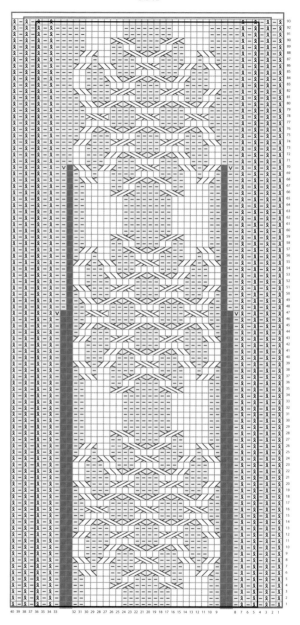

Tinker

A visit from the tinker is always an interesting event. He is a mender and an inventor, and may just have a little magic in his pockets along with his tools. These socks combine the practicality of the tinker in their simple style, with the inventiveness of a sideways construction and the magic of a delightful colorway peepling through.

SIZE CALCULATIONS:

This sock is constructed sideways so it is important to measure your stitch and row gauge. Use the following worksheet to determine your "foot number" of stitches.

My foot length = _____(A) inches.

Foot length - 2.5 inches = _____(B) inches.

Multiply (B) x 8 st/inch =_____ (C) stitches.

Subtract 12 from (C) = _____ (D). This is your foot number.

Cast on number = (D) + 66= _____ (E).

The charts for this pattern have red vertical lines denoting the spot where the markers are. Some sections of the chart have a variable number of stitches depending on what your "foot number" is. These sections have only a small representative number of stitches as a place holder.

CAST ON

With waste yarn, provisionally cast on (p. 115) (E) number of stitches from the worksheet above. (for women's size 7 we used 40 stitches (D) + 66 = 106 total).

PATTERN NOTES

Finished Circumference Measurements (un-stretched):

foot	ankle	mid calf
7.5 in	7.0 in	8.5 in

Yarn Used: Zitron **Trekking Pro Natura** (superwash wool/unprocessed bamboo) colors "*new mexico*" (color A) and "*near black*" (color B), 459 yards, 3.5 oz, 1 skein each.

WPI: 18

Needles: Straight needles or circulars in size to give correct gauge (2.5 mm –US size 1 suggested).

Gauge: 8 stitches / 10 rows per inch in stockinette knit flat.

Notions: 3 different markers, tapestry needle, waste yarn.

Color Suggestions: Painted, solid or semi-solid colors.

Sizing Notes: The size of this sock is calculated by you to fit your foot. To increase circumference add more color rows between black garter sections, or increase short rows.

Legend:
- ☐ K on RS, P on WS (color A)
- ☐ K on RS, P on WS (color B)
- ⊟ P on RS, K on WS (in established color)
- W wrap (in established color)

Chart 1

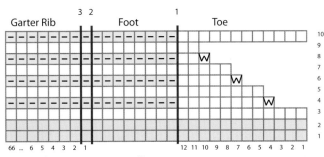

3 2   1

Garter Rib   Foot   Toe

66 ... 6 5 4 3 2 1   12 11 10 9 8 7 6 5 4 3 2 1

repeat this section for 66 stitches

repeat this section over your foot number of stitches

Chart 2

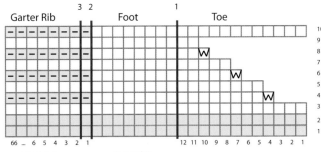

3 2   1

Garter Rib   Foot   Toe

66 ... 6 5 4 3 2 1   12 11 10 9 8 7 6 5 4 3 2 1

repeat this section for 66 stitches

repeat this section over your foot number of stitches

PLACE MARKERS

Set up rows

In waste yarn, K 1 row, placing markers as follows:

K12, place Marker 1, K foot number of stitches (D), place Marker 2, K1, place Marker 3, K to end.

INSTEP

Starting with color A, and beginning on WS with Row 2 (for the first repeat only), follow Chart 1 for 50 rows (5 repeats of Chart 1).

HEEL

Rows 1-16

Beginning of row - Marker 2: Follow Chart 2.

Marker 2 - Marker 3: Follow Chart 3.

Marker 3 - End of row: Follow Chart 2.

When Chart 3 is completed you should have 31 stitches between Markers 2 and 3.

Rows 17-34

Follow Chart 2 on all stitches for 18 rows.

Rows 35-50

Beginning of row - Marker 2: Follow Chart 2.

Marker 2 - Marker 3: Follow Chart 4.

Marker 3 - End of row: Follow Chart 2.

When Chart 4 is complete you should have 1 stitch between Markers 2 and 3.

Row 51:

Graft sides together in color A (this counts as Row 1 of the instep).

FINISHING

Sew toe together using mattress stitch. Weave in ends.

Chart 3   ## Chart 4

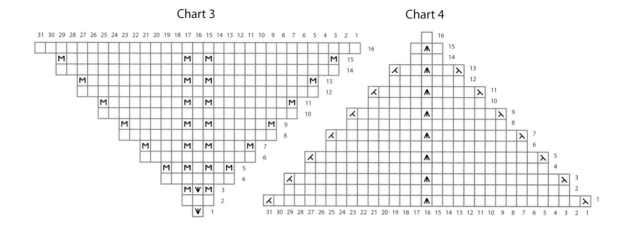

☐ K on RS, P on WS (in established color)

Ⓜ make 1, twisted

Ⓥ centered double increase

☒ K2 tog on RS, P2 tog on WS

☒ SSK on RS, SSP on WS

☒ centered double decrease

Galadriel

owerful and beautiful, Galadriel ruled over the Elven land of Lothlorien with wisdom and grace. Galadriel's power could be gentle, or formidable, depending on the circumstances. The Galadriel sock is at once both delicate and strong, with many options for different looks. Make some Galadriel socks for the gracious, powerful Queen in you!

Cast On

Cast on 24 stitches using the figure 8 cast on (12 loops on each needle = 24 stitches), knit one round.

Stitches are divided into two groups, instep stitches and heel stitches. (12 stitches each).

Toe

Round 1

    Instep stitches: K

    Heel stitches: K

Round 2

    Instep stitches: K1, M1, K to one stitch before end of instep stitches, M1, K1.

    Heel stitches: Repeat instep stitches.

Repeat Rounds 1 and 2 until you have 60 stitches total. Arrange to give 29 instep stitches and 31 heel stitches.

Foot

Continue to work each round in stockinette until sock measures 2.75 inches less than total foot length.

Pattern Notes

Finished Circumference Measurements (un-stretched):

foot	ankle	mid calf	upper calf
7.5 in	7.5 in	9.0 in	10.0 in

Yarn Used: Blue Moon Fiberarts **Socks That Rock** light weight (superwash merino) in color *"grawk"* (dark) or *"ghillie du"* (light), 380 yards, 4.5 oz, 2 skeins.

WPI: 16

Needles: DPNs or circulars in size to give correct gauge (2.75 mm –US size 2 suggested).

Gauge: 8 stitches / 11.5 rows per inch in stockinette knit in round.

Notions: 2 markers, 4 yards of ribbon, tapestry needle.

Color Suggestions: Solid or semi-solid colors.

Sizing Notes: Length of foot is measured by trying on sock. This pattern has a wide range of leg circumferences due to the lacing at the back of the sock.

HEEL FLAP

Work the first 6 heel stitches, place marker. These 6 heel stitches are called "side heel stitches." K the next 19 heel stitches. Turn work, leaving 6 side heel stitches on the other side. Slip first stitch, P across to marker. Turn work. Continue working back and forth across the center 19 stitches in stockinette, always slipping the first stitch, for 30 more rows. End having completed a WS row.

HEEL TURN

Turn heel

The heel turn is worked only on the center 19 heel stitches.

Row 1

K11, SSK, K1, turn.

Row 2

Slip first stitch, P4, P2 tog, P1, turn.

Row 3

Slip first stitch, K to 1 stitch before gap formed on previous row, SSK (this will include one stitch on each side of the gap), K1, turn.

Row 4

Slip first stitch, P to 1 stitch before gap formed on previous row, P2 tog (this will include one stitch on each side of the gap), P1, turn.

Repeat rows 3 and 4 until all of the center heel stitches have been worked. You should have 11 center heel stitches. End having completed a WS row.

GUSSET

Turn and K across heel stitches. Using heel stitch needle, pick up 16 stitches along side of heel flap, one in each slipped stitch plus one gap stitch. Add the 6 side heel stitches to the heel needle. K across instep stitches. Add the other 6 side heel stitches, pick up 16 stitches along flap, one in each slipped stitch plus one gap stitch, K to end of heel stitches. You now have 29 instep stitches and 55 heel stitches.

Round 1

Instep stitches: K

Heel stitches: K

Round 2

Instep stitches: K

Heel stitches: SSK, K to last 2 stitches, K2 tog.

Repeat Rounds 1 and 2, decreasing every other row on the heel stitches until you have 29 instep stitches and 31 heel stitches.

CUFF

Instep stitches: Follow Chart 1.

Heel stitches: K

When Chart 1 is complete, K the first 15 heel stitches, then begin Chart 2. Thereafter, the beginning of the round is in the center of the heel stitches. After Row 3 of Chart 2, work cuff back and forth, not in the round. When Chart 2 is complete, begin Chart 3. When Chart 3 is complete, begin bind off.

BIND OFF

Bind off using Elizabeth Zimmermann's sewn bind off (p. 123). Weave in ends. Lace ribbon through eyelets at back of sock, and tie at top.

Chart 2

Beginning at Row 3 work back and forth rather than in the round.

Chart 1

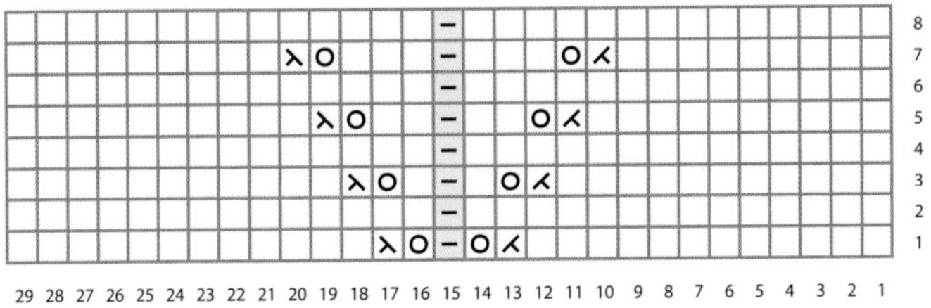

- no stitch
- K on RS, P on WS
- P on RS, K on WS
- YO
- K2 tog on RS, P2 tog on WS
- SSK on RS, SSP on WS
- K3 tog
- SSSK
- M1 purl
- M1 twisted

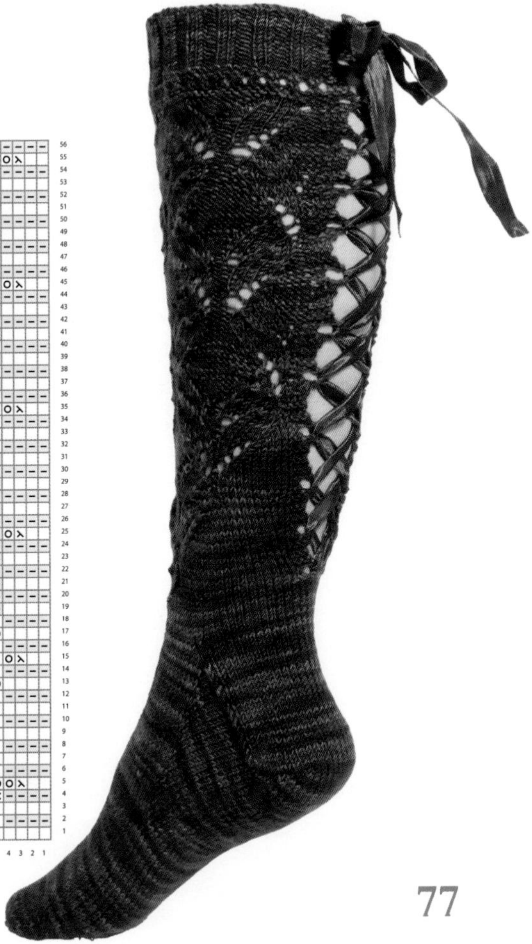

Chart 3

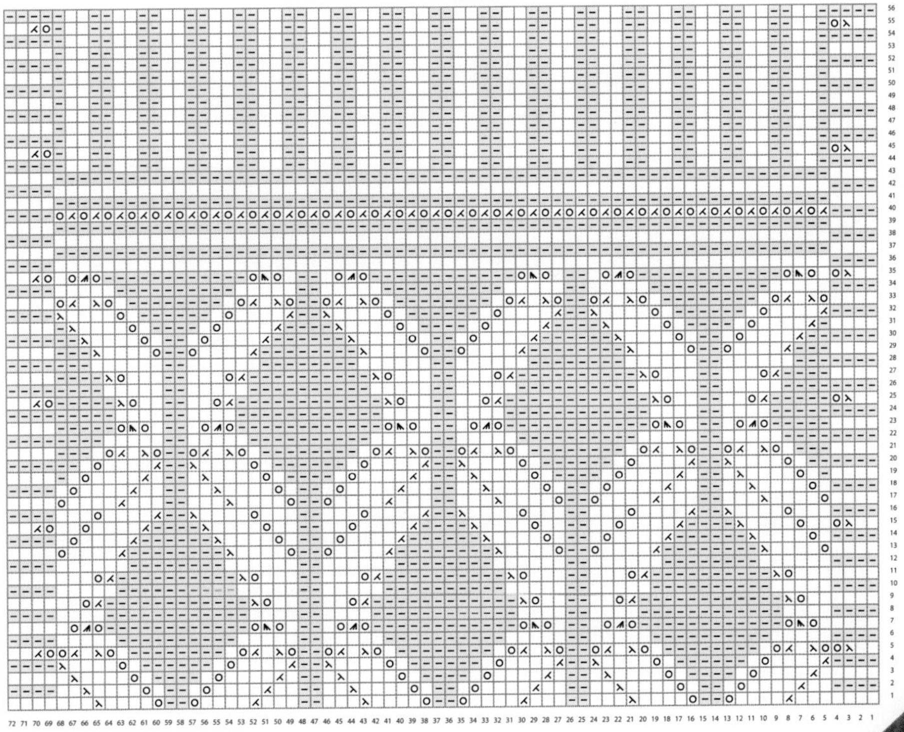

Traveler

ales of travelers reveal that caution is prudent when one is on the road. It is often wise to keep some things hidden, and where better to hide something than in a secret compartment? These socks have a concealed pocket for modern travelers to keep their treasures in, when out in the wide world.

NOTES: *This pattern may be knit with, or without beads. If you choose to knit with beads, begin each sock by stringing 9 beads onto your yarn. Slide the beads out of the way as you knit, then slide the beads into place as they are indicated on the charts. For more details about placement of beads, see p 120.*

Before casting on, wind 10 yards of yarn into a separate little ball.

Cast On

Cast on 64 stitches and join in the round, taking care not to twist your stitches.

Divide stitches into two groups; inside stitches (28 stitches) and outside stitches (36 stitches). These correspond to the inside of the leg and the outside of the leg, later you will rearrange them into instep and heel stitches.

Cuff

Ribbing:

P1, *K2, P2, repeat from *, end with K2, P1.

Work 2 rounds of ribbing before beginning chart.

Begin Chart 1

Round 1

   Inside stitches: P1, *K2, P2, repeat from *, end with K2, P1.

   Outside stitches: Follow Chart 1.

Pattern Notes

Finished Circumference Measurements (unstretched):

foot	ankle	mid calf
7.5 in	7.5 in	8.25 in

Yarn Used: Trekking XXL (superwash merino / nylon) in color *"284 tweed blues"*, 3.5 oz, 462 yds, 1 skein.

WPI: 17

Needles: DPNs or circulars in size to give correct gauge (2.75 mm –US size 2 suggested). One circular or set of DPNs in one size smaller for pocket.

Gauge: 8 stitches / 12 rows per inch in stockinette knit in round.

Notions: 18 6/0 beads, 2 coordinating buttons or extra large beads, cable needle, tapestry needle, crochet hook, waste yarn.

Color Suggestions: Solid/semi solid colors.

Sizing Notes: Length of foot is measured by trying on sock. This pattern is one size in circumference. To change sizes, increase or decrease needle size and yarn weight to get a different gauge.

Round 2

Inside stitches: Same as Round 1.

Outside stitches: P1, K2, P1. Place the next 28 stitches on a stitch holder.

Pocket

Using your smaller needle, provisionally cast on (p. 115) 28 stitches with waste yarn. Using the small 10 yard ball of yarn that you made in the beginning and smaller needles, pick up the 28 stitches from the holder and the provisional cast on (56 total) and knit in the round for 28 rounds. graft bottom of pocket.

Allow pocket to dangle on back side of your work. You will attach it at the end.

Continuing with main yarn, cast 14 stitches onto the outside stitch needle using crochet hook method (p. 116). Chain 10 to make button loop, cast on another 14 stitches with crochet hook. Continue with Chart 1, starting at stitch 33 and complete the round.

Rounds 4-7

Inside stitches: P1, *K2, P2, repeat from *, end with K2, P1.

Outside stitches: Follow Chart 1.

Round 8

Inside stitches: K5, M1 lifted, K18, M1 lifted, K5.

Outside stitches: Follow Chart 1.

You now have 30 inside stitches and 36 outside stitches.

Therefter work as follows:

Inside stitches: K

Outside stitches: Follow Chart 1.

When Chart 1 is completed you should have 30 inside stitches and 30 outside stitches.

Work 12 more rounds in plain stockinette.

HEEL

Rearrange stitches:

For Right leg: Move the last 15 outside stitches and the first 15 inside stitches to the instep stitches and the last 15 inside stitches and first 15 outside stitches to the heel stitches.

For Left leg: Move the first 15 outside stitches and the last 15 inside stitches to the instep stitches and the first 15 inside stitches and last 15 outside stitches to the heel stitches.

Working only the heel stitches, always slipping the first stitch of each row, and working back and forth, work K1 tbl, P1 ribbing for 30 rows or until the heel flap is the correct depth for your heel.

Turn heel:

Row 1

K18, SSK, K1, turn.

Row 2

Slip first stitch, P7, P2 tog, P1, turn.

Row 3

Slip first stitch, K to 1 stitch before gap formed on previous row, SSK (this will include one stitch on each side of the gap), K1, turn.

Row 4

Slip first stitch, P to 1 stitch before gap formed on previous row, P2 tog (this will include one stitch on each side of the gap), P1, turn.

Repeat Rows 3 and 4 until all side stitches have been worked. You should have 18 stitches on the heel needle. End having completed a WS row.

Gusset

Using heel stitch needle, pick up 16 stitches along side of heel flap. Work across instep, then pick up another 16 stitches on the other side of the flap. You now have 30 instep stitches and 50 heel stitches.

Round 1

Instep stitches: K

Heel stitches: K

Round 2

Instep stitches: K

Heel stitches: K1, SSK, K to last 3 stitches, K2 tog, K1.

Repeat Rounds 1 and 2 decreasing every other row on the heel stitches until you have 30 stitches per needle.

Foot

Instep stitches: K

Heel stitches: K

Repeat until foot is the correct length to begin toe shaping (usually this is at the base of the big toe).

Toe

Round 1

Instep stitches: K

Heel stitches: K

Round 2

Instep stitches: K1, SSK, K to last 3 stitches, K2 tog, K1.

Heel stitches: Repeat instep stitches.

Repeat Rounds 1 and 2 until you have 14 stitches per needle.

Close toe with Kitchener stitch (p. 124).

Attach Pocket

Remove the provisional cast on waste yarn from the outer edge of the pocket. Using a tapestry needle, sew the live stitches to the inside of your crocheted cast on edge.

Attach button to ribbing in correct spot for loop closure.

Chart 1

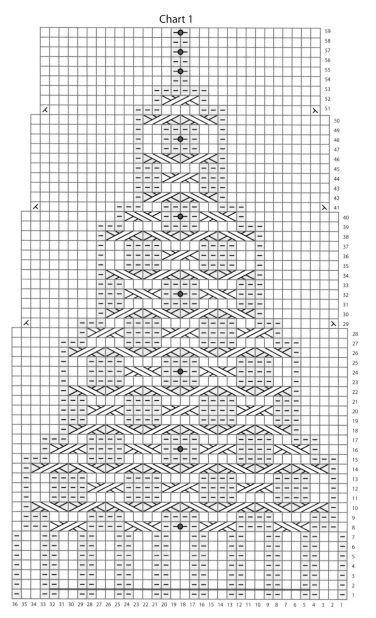

☐ K

⊟ P

◪ K2 tog

◪ SSK

⬤ place bead between 2 purl st

▨ 2 over 2 right knit cross

▧ 2 over 2 left knit cross

▨ 2 over 2 right purl cross

▧ 2 over 2 left purl cross

82

Mermaid

S panning the world of men, and the world of the sea, mermaids are enchanting in a both delightful and dangerous way. Luckily these socks will charm you without any fear of drowning. Although they look complicated, the stitch pattern is easy to learn and the charts will guide you through the transitions with confidence.

CAST ON

Cast on 72 stitches and join in the round, taking care not to twist your stitches.

Divide stitches evenly into two groups; instep stitches and heel stitches.

Notes: *Beads are placed on purl stitches as you work them using a crochet hook (p. 119).*

CUFF

K one round, P one round, K one round.

Begin Chart 1

Work following Chart 1. You will have 4 repeats of Chart 1 around the circumference of the cuff.

Begin Chart 2

When Chart 1 is completed, work following Chart 2. You will have 6 repeats of Chart 2 around the circumference of the cuff. When Chart 2 is complete, begin Chart 3.

Begin Chart 3

   Instep stitches: Follow Chart 2 beginning at Row 16 and working through 43, then start again at Row 16 and work through 31.

   Heel stitches: Follow Chart 3 beginning at Row 1.

PATTERN NOTES

Finished Circumference Measurements (un-stretched):

foot	ankle	mid calf	upper calf
7.0 in	6.5 in	8.0 in	9.0 in

Yarn Used: Malabrigo **Sock** (superwash merino) in color *"809 Solis"*, 440 yds, 3.5 oz, 2 skeins.

WPI: 17

Needles: DPNs or circulars in size to give correct gauge (3.25 mm –US size 3 suggested).

Gauge: 7.5 stitches / 10.5 rows per inch in stockinette knit in round.

Notions: 40 beads, size 12 steel crochet hook, tapestry needle.

Color Suggestions: Painted or solid/semi solid colors.

Sizing Notes: Length of foot is measured by trying on sock. This pattern is one size in circumference. To change sizes, increase or decrease needle size and yarn weight to get a different gauge.

Begin Chart 4

When Chart 3 is completed,

> **Instep stitches:** Follow Chart 4 through Row 30.

> **Heel stitches***:* Continue in twisted ribbing stitch as established.

When you have completed Row 30 of Chart 4, move 2 stitches from the beginning and 3 stitches from the end of the instep stitches to the heel stitches. You should now have 33 heel stitches and 31 instep stitches.

HEEL

Working only the heel stitches, always slipping the first stitch of each row, and working back and forth, work K1 tbl, P1 ribbing for 30 rows or until the heel flap is the correct depth for your heel.

Turn heel:

Row 1

> K19, SSK, K1, turn.

Row 2

> Slip first stitch, P5, P2 tog, P1, turn.

Row 3

> Slip first stitch, K to 1 stitch before gap formed on previous row, SSK (this will include one stitch on each side of the gap), K1, turn.

Row 4

> Slip first stitch, P to 1 stitch before gap formed on previous row, P2 tog (this will include one stitch on each side of the gap), P1, turn.

Repeat Rows 3 and 4 until all side stitches have been worked. You should have 19 stitches on the heel needle. End having completed a WS row.

GUSSET

Using heel stitch needle, pick up 16 stitches along side of heel flap, work Row 31 of Chart 4 on instep, then pick up another 16 stitches on the other side of the flap. You now have 31 instep stitches and 51 heel stitches.

Round 1

> **Instep stitches:** Continue with Chart 4 beginning at Row 32.

> **Heel stitches:** K

Round 2

> **Instep stitches:** Continue with Chart 4.

> **Heel stitches:** K1, SSK, K to last 3 stitches, K2 tog, K1.

Repeat Rounds 1 and 2 until Chart 4 is finished. Thereafter continue in the same fashion, working K1 tbl, P1 ribbing as established on the instep stitches and decreasing every other row on the heel stitches until you have 31 stitches per needle.

Chart 1

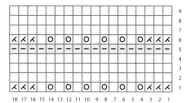

Chart 2

Chart 3

Foot

Instep stitches: Continue working in K1 tbl, P1 ribbing as established.

Heel stitches: Continue in plain stockinette.

Repeat until foot is the correct length to begin toe shaping (usually this is at the base of the big toe).

Toe

Round 1

Instep stitches: K

Heel stitches: K

Round 2

Instep stitches: K1, SSK, K to last 3 stitches, K2 tog, K1.

Heel stitches: Repeat instep stitches.

Repeat Rounds 1 and 2 until you have 15 stitches per needle.

Close toe with Kitchener stitch (p. 124).

Chart 4

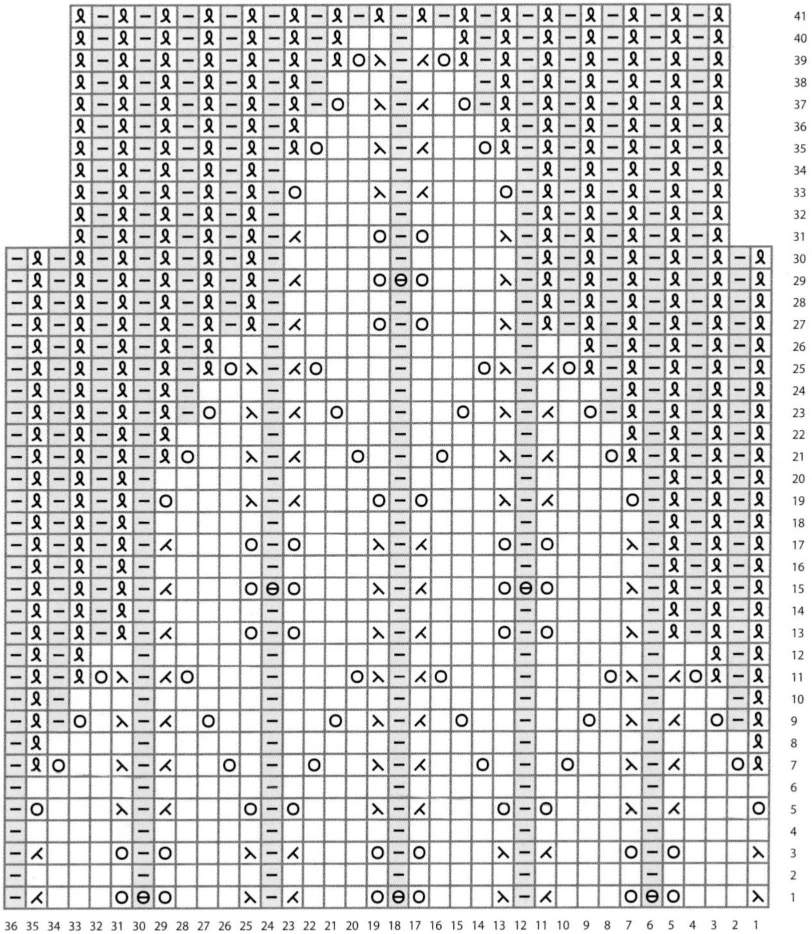

- no stitch
- K
- P
- YO
- K2 tog
- SSK
- K tbl
- place bead with crochet hook then purl

Alchemist

 *he Alchemist uses his magic and science to turn one thing into another. Is it lead or is it gold? These socks have an alchemy all their own, from the shading of the yarn to the eye dazzling tesselations, you're never quite sure what you're looking at, is it dark on light or light on dark? Make a pair of Alchemist stockings when you need a little magic, or science.*

CAST ON

Cast on 92 stitches in color A and join in the round, taking care not to twist your stitches. Stitches are divided into two groups, instep stitches and heel stitches. Arrange stitches so that the end of the round occurs in the center of the heel stitches.

CUFF

Ribbing

Work 8 rounds of K2 tbl, P2 ribbing in color A.

Set up round

K 1 round, increasing evenly by 8 stitches. You now have 100 stitches.

Begin Chart 1

Work following Chart 1.

When Chart 1 is completed, begin heel. You should have 63 stitches. Break yarn.

HEEL

Rearrange stitches:

Move last instep stitch to beginning of heel stitches. You now have 30 instep stitches and 33 heel stitches.

Heel flap:

Working only the heel stitches, always slipping the first stitch of each row, and working back and forth, follow Chart 2. When Chart 2 is completed, turn heel.

PATTERN NOTES

Finished Circumference Measurements (unstretched):

foot	ankle	mid calf	upper calf
8.0 in	8.0 in	11.0 in	12.75

Yarn Used: Schoppel Wolle **Zauberball** (wool/nylon) color "*stonewashed*" (color A) and "*schatten*" (color B), 3.5 oz, 400 yards, 1 skein each.

WPI: 18

Needles: DPNs or circulars in size to give correct gauge (2.5 mm –US size 1 suggested).

Gauge: 8 stitches / 11 rows per inch in stockinette knit in round.

Notions: Tapestry needle.

Color Suggestions: Painted, solid or semi-solid colors.

Sizing Notes: Length of foot is measured by trying on sock. This pattern is one size in circumference. To change sizes, increase or decrease needle size and yarn weight to get a different gauge. Because colorwork has little elasticity, unstretched circumferences are larger.

Turn heel:

Heel turn is worked only in color B.

Row 1

K18, SSK, K1, turn.

Row 2

Slip first stitch, P4, P2 tog, P1, turn.

Row 3

Slip first stitch, K to 1 stitch before gap formed on previous row, SSK (this will include one stitch on each side of the gap), K1, turn.

Row 4

Slip first stitch, P to 1 stitch before gap formed on previous row, P2 tog (this will include one stitch on each side of the gap), P1, turn.

Repeat Rows 3 and 4 until all side stitches have been worked. You should have 19 stitches on the heel needle. End having completed a RS row.

GUSSET

Using heel stitch needle, pick up 16 stitches along side of heel flap in the color pattern of Chart 3.

Work across instep stitches following in the color pattern of Chart 3.

Pick up another 16 stitches on the other side of the heel flap, following Chart 3.

Work across remaining heel stitches following color pattern of Chart 3.

You now have 30 instep stitches and 51 heel stitches.

Round 1

Setup: Move first heel stitch to end of instep stitches. You now have 31 instep sttiches and 50 heel stitches.

Instep stitches: K, following Chart 3 (instep).

Heel stitches: K, following Chart 3 (heel).

FOOT

When Chart 3 is completed you will have 31 instep stitches and 33 heel stitches.

Instep stitches: K following Chart 4.

Heel stitches: K following Chart 4.

Repeat until foot is the correct length to begin toe shaping (usually this is at the base of the big toe).

Chart 2

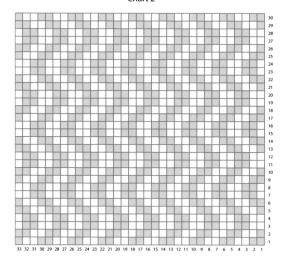

Chart 1

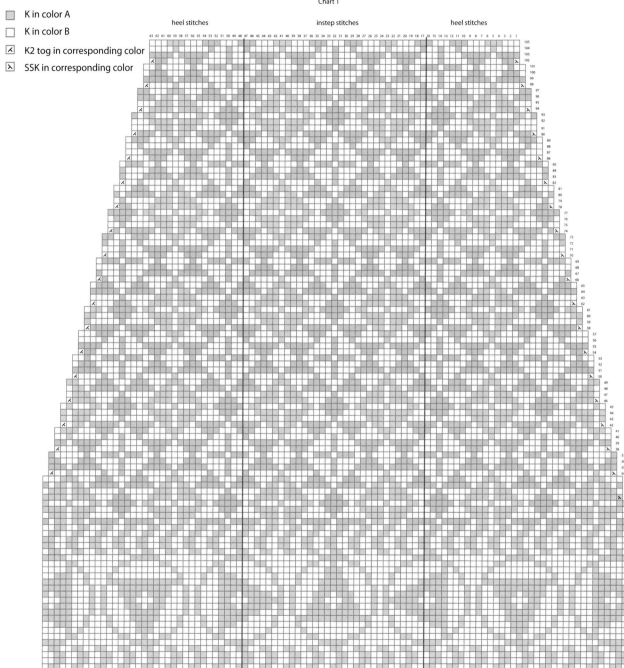

Chart 3 heel

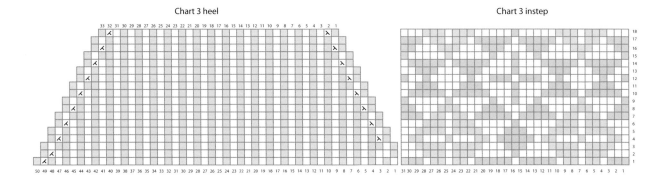

Chart 3 instep

Chart 4

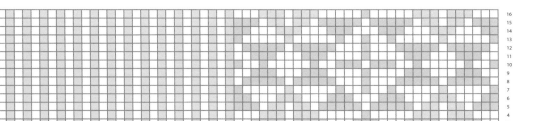

Chart 5

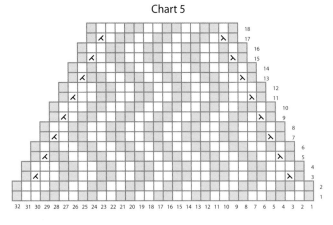

TOE

Rearrange stitches:

Move last instep stitch back to beginning of heel stitches. You now have 32 instep stitches and 32 heel stitches.

Instep stitches: K following Chart 5.

Heel stitches: Repeat instep stitches.

When Chart 5 is complete, close toe with Kitchener stitch (p. 124).

Atlantis

 shining city on the edge of the sea, Atlantis was the mythical home of an ancient and wise race. The mysteries of Atlantis have been lost in the mists of time, and all traces of that beautiful city have vanished. These Atlantis socks are reminiscent of a city by the sea; make some Atlantis socks when you feel the desire for a little beauty, or wisdom.

Cast On

Cast on 24 stitches using the figure 8 cast on (12 loops = 24 stitches), knit one round.

Stitches are divided into two groups, instep stitches and heel stitches (12 stitches each).

Toe

Round 1

Instep stitches: K

    Heel stitches: K

Round 2

    Instep stitches: K1, M1, K to one stitch before end of instep stitches, M1, K1.

    Heel stitches: Repeat instep stitches.

Repeat Rounds 1 and 2 until you have 60 stitches total (30 instep stitches, 30 heel stiches).

Foot

Begin Chart 1

    Instep stitches: Follow Chart 1. You will have 3 repeats of the chart across the instep stitches.

    Heel stitches: K

Continue working foot, repeating Chart 1 as necessary, until sock measures 2.75 inches less than total foot length.

Pattern Notes

Finished Circumference Measurements (unstretched):

foot	ankle	mid calf
7.25 in	7.25 in	7.25 in

Yarn Used: Madeline Tosh **Tosh Sock** (superwash merino) color "*iceburg*", 395 yards, 1 skein.

WPI: 15

Needles: DPNs or circulars in size to give correct gauge (2.75 mm –US size 2 suggested).

Gauge: 8 stitches / 11 rows per inch in stockinette knit in round.

Notions: Tapestry needle.

Color Suggestions: Painted, solid / semi-solid colors.

Sizing Notes: Length of foot is measured by trying on sock. This pattern is one size in circumference. To change sizes, increase or decrease needle size and yarn weight to get a different gauge.

Heel Flap

Work the first 6 heel stitches, place marker. These 6 heel stitches are called "side heel stitches." K the next 18 heel stitches. Turn work, leaving 6 side heel stitches on the other side. Slip first stitch, P across to marker. Turn work. Continue working back and forth across the center 18 stitches in stockinette, always slipping the first stitch, for 30 rows. End having completed a WS row.

Heel Turn

Turn heel

The heel turn is worked only on the center 18 heel stitches.

Row 1

K10, SSK, K1, turn.

Row 2

Slip first stitch, P3, P2 tog, P1, turn.

Row 3

Slip first stitch, K to 1 stitch before gap formed on previous row, SSK (this will include one stitch on each side of the gap), K1, turn.

Row 4

Slip first stitch, P to 1 stitch before gap formed on previous row, P2 tog (this will include one stitch on each side of the gap), P1, turn.

Repeat Rows 3 and 4 until all side stitches have been worked. You should have 10 center heel stitches. End having completed a WS row.

Gusset

Work across heel stitches in stockinette. Using heel stitch needle, pick up 16 stitches along side of heel flap, one in each slipped stitch plus one gap stitch. Add the 6 side heel stitches to the heel needle. Work across instep stitches following Chart 1. Add the other 6 side heel stitches, pick up 16 stitches along flap, one in each slipped stitch plus one gap stitch, K to end of heel stitches. You will have 30 instep stitches and 54 heel stitches.

Round 1

Instep stitches: Work following Chart 1.

Heel stitches: K

Round 2

Instep stitches: Work following Chart 1.

Heel stitches: SSK, K to last 2 stitches, K2 tog.

Repeat Rounds 1 and 2, decreasing every other row on the heel stitches until you have 30 instep stitches and 30 heel stitches.

Cuff

Instep stitches: Continue following Chart 1.

Heel stitches: Follow Chart 1 beginning at the same row that you are working on the instep stitches.

Repeat the chart from the beginning, if necessary, until the cuff measures 2 inches.

Begin Chart 2

Follow Chart 2 until chart is complete.

Work 8 rounds of K2, P2 ribbing.

Bind Off

Bind off using Elizabeth Zimmermann's sewn bind off (p. 123). Weave in ends.

Legend

☐	K
−	P
⊙	YO
⟋	K2 tog
⟍	SSK
⋀	centered double decrease

Chart 1

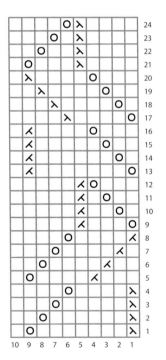

Chart 2

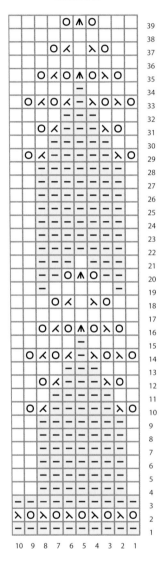

Firebird

The firebird is a mystical creature whose brilliant red plumage glows with the intensity of a bonfire. Just one tailfeather from the firebird is enough to light an entire room. The firebird flies around the land spreading hope and beauty. Woe to those who might try to capture it! The firebird socks can also light up a room with just a few feathers.

CAST ON

Cast on 99 stitches with color A and join in the round, taking care not to twist your stitches.

CUFF

Ribbing:

Join color B and work following Chart 1 Left for left sock or Chart 1 Right for right sock..

When Chart 1 is completed, begin heel. You should have 64 stitches.

HEEL

Set up round:

Rearrange stitches to make 2 sets of stitches, instep stitches and heel stitches. Stitches 1-16 are heel stitches. Stitches 17-48 are instep stitches. Stitches 49-64 are heel stitches. Break yarn.

Heel flap:

Starting at first heel stitch, Follow Chart 2.

Turn heel:

Notes: The heel turn is worked only in color A.

Row 1

K18, SSK, K1, turn.

Row 2

Slip first stitch, P5, P2 tog, P1, turn.

PATTERN NOTES

Finished Circumference Measurements (unstretched):

foot	ankle	mid calf	upper calf
7.5 in	7.5 in	9.0 in	10.0 in

Yarn Used: Blue Moon Fiberarts **Socks That Rock** light weight (superwash merino) in color "*shadow*" (color A) and color "*just right red*" (color B), 380 yards, 4.5 oz, 2 skeins each.

WPI: 16

Needles: DPNs or circulars in size to give correct gauge (2.75 mm –US size 2 suggested).

Gauge: 9 stitches / 10 rows per inch in stockinette knit in round.

Notions: 2 markers, tapestry needle.

Color Suggestions: Solid or semi-solid colors.

Sizing Notes: Length of foot is measured by trying on sock. This pattern is one size in circumference. To change sizes, increase or decrease needle size and yarn weight to get a different gauge.

Row 3

Slip first stitch, K to 1 stitch before gap formed on previous row, SSK (this will include one stitch on each side of the gap), K1, turn.

Row 4

Slip first stitch, P to 1 stitch before gap formed on previous row, P2 tog (this will include one stitch on each side of the gap), P1, turn.

Repeat Rows 3 and 4 until all side stitches have been worked. You should have 18 stitches on the heel needle. End having completed a WS row.

GUSSET

Work across heel stitches in color A, using heel stitch needle, pick up 16 stitches along side of heel flap beginning with color A and alternating colors every stitch to make a 1x1 stripe pattern.

Work across instep stitches following Chart 3, then, pick up another 16 stitches on the other side of the heel flap in 1x1 color stripe pattern beginning with color B. Work across the next 32 heel stitches following Chart 3, work rest of heel stitches in color pattern as established.

You now have 32 instep stitches and 50 heel stitches.

Round 1

Instep stitches: Continue to follow Chart 3.

Heel stitches: While working in stripe pattern as established from Chart 3, work 14, place Marker 1, work 22, place Marker 2, work 14.

Round 2

Instep stitches: Continue following Chart 3.

Heel stitches: While working in stripe pattern from Chart 3, work 14, slip marker, SSK, work to last 2 stitches, before Marker 2, K2 tog, slip marker, work 14.

Repeat Rounds 1 and 2, decreasing every other round on the heel stitches until you have 32 instep stitches and 32 heel stitches.

Instep stitches: Continue following color pattern as established in Chart 3.

Heel stitches: While following stripe pattern as established, work 14, SSK, work to end of row.

FOOT

Continue working in color pattern as established in Chart 3 until foot is 2 inches from the end.

TOE

Instep stitches: Work from red line forward on Chart 3.

Heel stitches: Work from red line forward on Chart 3.

When Chart 3 is completed, close toe with Kitchener stitch (p. 124).

Reverse colors and chart on second sock.

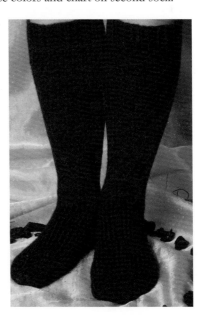

Chart 1 (Left)

- K in color A
- K in color B
- K2 tog in corresponding color
- SSK in corresponding color

Chart 1 (Right)

101

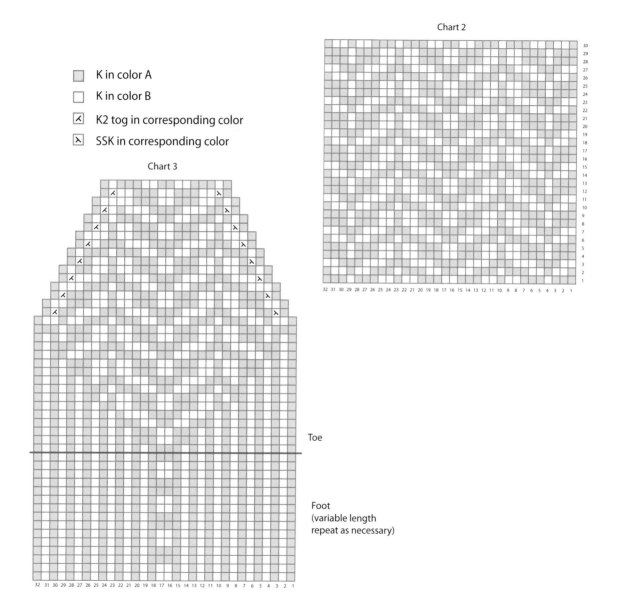

K in color A

K in color B

K2 tog in corresponding color

SSK in corresponding color

Chart 3

Chart 2

Toe

Foot
(variable length
repeat as necessary)

Talking Fish

f you happen to catch a talking fish, it is best to spare his life and throw him back. A grateful talking fish will probably bring you riches, good luck, or at least grant you a few wishes. This talking fish loves the ripples of the watery river, and brings the good luck of a flattering fit, and the charm of a painted skein shown off to maximum effect. Your fishes will be the talk of the town.

SIZE CALCULATIONS

This sock is constructed sideways so it is important to measure your stitch and row gauge. Use the following worksheet to determine your "foot number" of stitches.

My foot length = _____(A) inches.

Foot length - 2.5 inches = _____(B) inches.

Multiply (B) x 8 st/inch =_____ (C) stitches.

Subtract 12 from (C) = _____ (D). This is your foot number. Add stitches to (or subtract from) (D) until it is a multiple of 17 = _____(E).

Cast on number = (E) + 56 = _____ (F).

The charts for this pattern have red vertical lines denoting the spot where the markers are. Some sections of the chart have a variable number of stitches depending on what your "foot number" is. These sections have only a small representative number of stitches as a place holder. On the instep you will repeat the 17 stitch pattern within these sections, continuing in pattern as you move from the section between Markers 1 and 2 to the section between Markers 2 and 4, noting where Marker 3 lands within the pattern. On the heel pick up the pattern at Marker 3 in the same spot as on the instep.

PATTERN NOTES

Finished Circumference Measurements (un-stretched):

foot	ankle
8.5 inches	8.5 inches

Yarn Used: Enchanted Knoll Farm **Superwash Sock Yarn** (superwash merino / nylon) in color *"sedona"*, 435 yards, 3.5 oz, 1 skein.

WPI: 17

Needles: Straights or circulars in size to give correct gauge (2.75 mm –US size 2 suggested).

Gauge: 8 stitches / 11 rows per inch in stockinette knit flat.

Notions: 4 markers, tapestry needle, waste yarn.

Color Suggestions: Painted, solid or semi-solid colors.

Sizing Notes: This sock is calculated by you to fit your foot. To increase circumference add more pattern rows before heel increase and before heel decrease.

Cast On

With waste yarn, provisionally cast on (p. 115) (F) number of stitches from the worksheet above. (For women's size 7 we used 51 stitches (E) + 56 = 107 total).

Place Markers

Set up rows

In waste yarn, K 1 row, placing markers as follows:

K12, place Marker 1, K foot number of stitches (D), place Marker 2, K1, place Marker 3, K until 10 stitches remain, place marker 4, K to end. Purl back in waste yarn.

Instep

Follow Chart 1 for 48 rows (6 repeats of Chart 1).

Heel

Rows 1-16

Beginning of row - Marker 2: Follow Chart 2.

Marker 2 - Marker 3: Follow Chart 3.

Marker 3 - End of row: Follow Chart 2.

You should now have 31 stitches between Markers 2 and 3.

Rows 17-31:

When Chart 3 is complete, follow Chart 2 on all stitches for 15 rows. Stitches between Markers 2 and 3 are worked in stockinette.

Rows 32-47:

Beginning of row - Marker 2: Follow Chart 2.

Marker 2 - Marker 3: Follow Chart 4.

Marker 3 - End of row: Follow Chart 2.

You should now have 1 stitch between Markers 2 and 3.

Row 48:

Graft sides together using Kitchener stitch (p. 124).

Finishing

Sew toe together. Weave in ends.

Chart 1

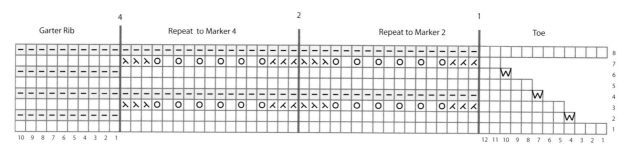

Chart 2

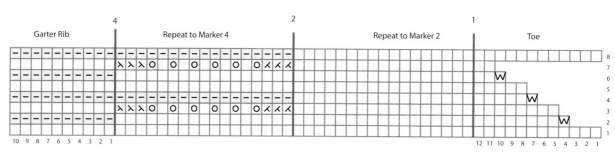

Chart 3   Chart 4

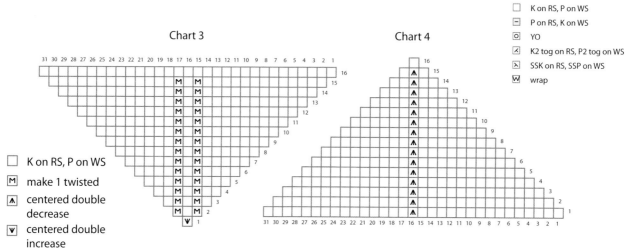

	K on RS, P on WS
−	P on RS, K on WS
⊙	YO
⊼	K2 tog on RS, P2 tog on WS
⅄	SSK on RS, SSP on WS
W	wrap

	K on RS, P on WS
M	make 1 twisted
⋏	centered double decrease
⋎	centered double increase

Tree of Life

he Tree of Life shows up in many cultures, myths, philosophies and religions and reminds us that we are all interconnected with each other, we are rooted with the earth and our branches reach out to every living being. Make some tree of life socks to forge new roots, to remind yourself of your own connections, or just to bask in the serenity of their branches!

Cast On

Cast on 76 stitches in color A and join in the round, taking care not to twist your stitches.

Cuff

Ribbing:

In color A, work 10 rounds of K1 tbl, P1 ribbing. Work one round of K, increasing by 13 stitches evenly spaced to end up with 89 stitches total.

Begin Chart 1

Join color B.

Work following Chart 1 ending at stitch 47 as indicated on the chart.

When Chart 1 is completed, begin heel. You should have 63 stitches.

Heel

Set up round:

Rearrange stitches to make 2 sets of stitches, instep stitches and heel stitches as marked on chart. Stitches 1-16 are heel stitches. Stitches 17-47 are instep stitches. Stitches 48-63 are heel stitches.

You now have 31 instep stitches and 32 heel stitches.

Pattern Notes

Finished Circumference Measurements (unstretched):

foot	ankle	mid calf
7.5 in	7.5 in	9.0 in

Yarn Used: Blue and Black version: Malabrigo **Sock** (superwash merino) in color (A) "*black*" and color (B) "*indiecita*", 440 yards, 3.5 oz, 1 skein each.
Red and Gold version: Lisa Souza Dyeworks **Sock!** (superwash wool/nylon) in color (A) "*garnet*" and color (B) "*petroglyph*", 450 yards, 4.0 oz, 1 skein each.

WPI: 17

Needles: DPNs or circulars in size to give correct gauge (2.75 mm –US size 2 suggested).

Gauge: 10 stitches / 10 rows per inch in 2 color stranded stockinette knit in round.

Notions: 2 markers, tapestry needle.

Color Suggestions: One solid or semi-solid and a second solid or painted yarn in contrasting colors.

Sizing Notes: Length of foot is measured by trying on sock. This pattern is one size in circumference. To change sizes, increase or decrease needle size and yarn weight to get a different gauge.

Heel flap:

Working only the heel stitches, always slipping the first stitch of each row, and working back and forth, follow Chart 2. When Chart 2 is completed, turn heel.

Turn heel:

Notes: The heel turn is worked only in color A.

Row 1

K18, SSK, K1, turn.

Row 2

Slip first stitch, P5, P2 tog, P1, turn.

Row 3

Slip first stitch, K to 1 stitch before gap formed on previous row, SSK (this will include one stitch on each side of the gap), K1, turn.

Row 4

Slip first stitch, P to 1 stitch before gap formed on previous row, P2 tog (this will include one stitch on each side of the gap), P1, turn.

Repeat Rows 3 and 4 until all side stitches have been worked. You should have 18 stitches on the heel needle. End having completed a WS row.

GUSSET

Work across heel stitches alternating colors every stitch to make a 1x1 color stripe pattern beginning with color B. Using heel stitch needle, pick up 16 stitches along side of heel flap continuing in the 1x1 color stripe pattern.

Work across instep stitches in 1x1 color stripe pattern beginning with color A.

Pick up another 16 stitches on the other side of the heel flap in 1x1 color stripe pattern beginning with color B. Work across the next 8 heel stitches in 1x1 stripe pattern. K2 tog, work to the end of the heel stitches in 1x1 stripe pattern.

You now have 31 instep stitches and 49 heel stitches and beginning of round is now at the first instep stitch.

Round 1

Instep stitches: Continue to work in 1x1 color stripe pattern.

Heel stitches: While working in stripe pattern, work 14, place Marker 1, work 21, place Marker 2, work 14.

Round 2

Instep stitches: Continue working in 1x1 color stripe pattern.

Heel stitches: While working in stripe pattern, work 14, slip marker, SSK, work to last 2 stitches, before Marker 2, K2 tog, slip marker, work 14.

Repeat Rounds 1 and 2, decreasing every other round on the heel stitches until you have 31 instep stitches and 31 heel stitches.

FOOT

Continue working in color pattern as established until foot measures 5" less than desired length.

Work Chart 3 Rounds 1 through 24.

TOE

Instep stitches: Follow Chart 3 from Round 25 onward.

Heel stitches: Repeat instep stitches.

When Chart 3 is complete, close toe with Kitchener stitch (p. 124).

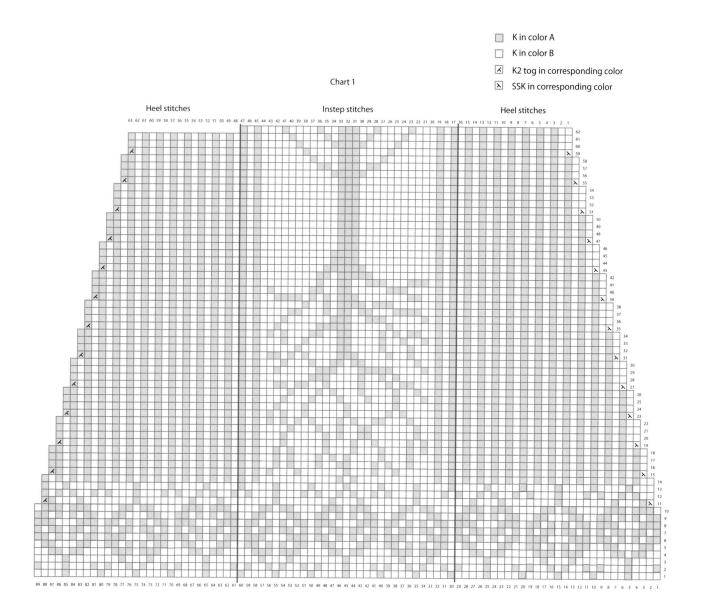

Chart 1

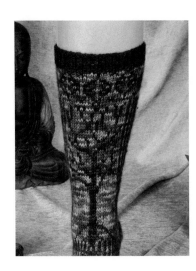

Chart 3

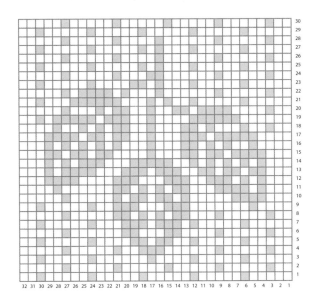

Chart 2

☐ color A
☐ color B

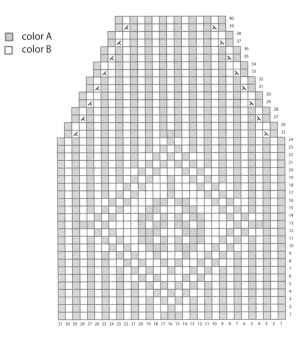

Glossary

Abbreviations and Symbols

K	knit	K2 tog	knit 2 together
P	purl	SSK	slip, slip, knit
K tbl	knit through back loop	SSSK	slip, slip, slip, knit
M1	make 1 (followed by the method)	K3 tog	knit 3 together
YO	yarn over		

■	no stitch	⊟⊟	cluster over k and p
☐	knit	⊟⊟⊟⊟	cluster over kppk
⊟	purl	⟋	1 over 1 right purl cross
⅄	knit thru back loop	⟍	1 over 1 left purl cross
ⱱ	make 1 purl	⟋	1 over 1 right knit cross
M	make 1	⟍	1 over 1 left knit cross
O	yarn over	⟍⟍	2 over 1 right purl cross
⟋	K2 tog	⟍⟍	2 over 1 left purl cross
⟍	SSK	⟍⟍	2 over 1 right knit cross
⋀	centered double dec.	⟍⟍	2 over 1 left knit cross
⟍	SSSK	⟍⟍	2 over 2 right purl cross
⟋	K3 tog	⟍⟍	2 over 2 left purl cross
B	bind of f one sttch	⟍⟍	2 over 2 right knit cross
W	wrap and turn	⟍⟍	2 over 2 left knit cross
⊖	place bead with ⊠ crochet hook on⊠ purl stitch	⊡	inline bead placement ⊠ between two purl stitches

Slip Knot Cast On

Make a slip knot at the end of the yarn and place on needle (no need for a long tail).

Make a backwards loop and place on needle.

Hold tension on the loop.

Dip needle down and scoop up tail and pull through loop.

Move loop to snug up against previous loop. Hold index finger against the back of the newly forming stitch and keep tension on it.

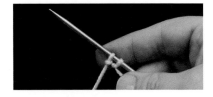

Cinch up the stitch onto the needle keeping tension on the back of the stitch with your forefinger.

A row of slip knot cast on stitches.

Crochet Cast On
(Also Provisional Cast On)

Place slip knot on crochet hook.

Wrap yarn clockwise around needle.

Pull yarn up and through the slip knot loop.

Move working yarn from front of needle to back of needle.

Again pull yarn up and through loop.

A row of crochet cast on.

If you are using the crochet cast on as a provisional cast on, crochet a few extra stitches at the end, cut yarn and pull through last loop. When it is time to remove your provisional cast on, this is the end you will pull from.

Figure 8 Cast On

Hold end of yarn and begin to wrap yarn around needles in a figure 8.

Continue winding around needles in a figure 8 until you have the right number of loops on each needle.

Knit off the loops entering the stitch from the left.

Turn your work and knit the other half of the loops off through the back loop.

Knit Stitch (K)

Holding yarn in back, enter stitch from left hand side, pull yarn through.

Knit through the back loop (Ktbl)

Holding yarn in back, enter stitch from right hand side, pull yarn through.

Purl Stitch (P)

Holding yarn in front, enter stitch from right hand side, pull yarn through.

Left Leaning Decrease (SSK)

Slip two stitches off left needle, knitwise, one at a time.

Knit both stitches together through the back loop.

Right Leaning Decrease (K2 tog)

Enter both stitches together from the left hand side.

Knit both stitches together.

Centered Double Decrease

Slip two stitches knitwise together from the left needle to the right needle. (From WS, slip two stitches purlwise together from the left needle to the right needle)

Knit (or purl on purl side) the next stitch.

Pass the two slipped stitches together over the stitch you just knitted (purled).

Your decrease will be centered.

Left Leaning Double Decrease (SSSK)

Slip three stitches off left needle, knitwise, one at a time.

Knit all three stitches together through the back loop.

Right Leaning Double Decrease (K3 tog)

Enter all three stitches together from the left hand side.

Knit all three stitches together.

Centered Double Increase

K1, P1, K1 into the same stitch.

Yarn Over

Bring yarn over needle from front to back.

Knit the next stitch.

An extra stitch is made, with a hole beneath it.

Make 1 Below

Pick up stitch below.

Knit into the stitch you picked up.

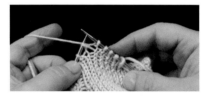

An extra stitch is made between sttiches, without making a hole.

Make 1 Twisted

Pick up bar between stitches.

Knit into the back loop of the stitch.

An extra stitch is made with no hole beneath it.

Make 1 Lifted

Pick up the bar between stitches.

Knit into the bar, making an extra stitch with a small hole below it.

Make 1 Purl

Purl into the front loop of the stitch, do not slip stitch off needle.

Purl into the back loop of the stitch.

An extra stitch is made with no hole below.

The extra stitch becomes nearly invisible when in the midst of a purl field.

Clustered Stitches

Move the stitches to be clustered to a cable needle.

Wrap your working yarn around the cable needle counter clockwise, twice.

Work the clustered stitches according to the underlying stitch noted on the chart.

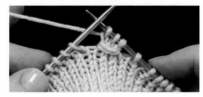

Clustered stitches.

Inline Bead Placement

String beads onto yarn ahead of time. Slide beads out of the way as you knit.

When you come to the spot indicated on the chart for placing a bead, work the first stitch (a purl), then slide the bead all the way up next to the stitch worked.

Work the next stitch (a purl).

Bead sits on the bar nestled between two purl stitches.

119

Bead Placement with a Crochet Hook

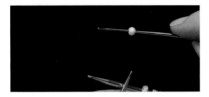

When you get to the spot indicated on the chart for a bead to be placed, put the bead on a small crochet hook.

Pick up the stitch the bead is to be placed on.

Gently pull the stitch through the bead.

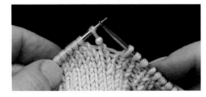

Place the stitch back on the left hand needle.

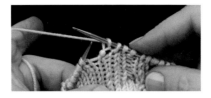

Knit (or purl) the stitch as usual. The bead will be embedded in your knittting directly on a stitch.

2 over 2 Left Knit Cross

Place 2 stitches on a cable needle held in front of your work.

Knit the next 2 stitches.

Slip the stitches from the cable needle back to the left hand needle.

Knit the two slipped stitches off.

2 Over 1 Left Purl Cross

Place 2 stitches on a cable needle held in front of your work. Purl the next 1 stitch. Slip the stitches from the cable needle back to the left hand needle. Knit the two slipped stitches off.

1 Over 1 Left Knit Cross

Place 1 stitch on a cable needle held in front of your work. knit the next 1 stitch. Slip the stitch from the cable needle back to the left hand needle and knit the slipped stitch off.

1 Over 1 Left Purl Cross

Place 1 stitch on a cable needle held in front of your work. Purl the next 1 stitch. Slip the stitch from the cable needle back to the left hand needle and knit the slipped stitch off.

2 Over 2 Right Knit Cross

Place 2 stitches on a cable needle held in back of work.

Knit the next 2 stitches.

Slip stitches from cable needle back to left hand needle.

Knit the 2 stitches off.

2 Over 1 Right Purl Cross

Place 1 stitch on a cable needle held in back of your work. Knit the next 2 stitches. Slip the stitch from the cable needle back to the left hand needle. Purl the slipped stitch off.

1 Over 1 Right Knit Cross

Place 1 stitch on a cable needle held in back of your work. knit the next 1 stitch. Slip the stitch from the cable needle back to the left hand needle and knit the slipped stitch off.

1 Over 1 Right Purl Cross

Place 1 stitch on a cable needle held in back of your work. Knit the next 1 stitch. Slip the stitch from the cable needle back to the left hand needle and purl the slipped stitch off.

Wrap and Turn

If you're wrapping on the knit side of the sock, bring yarn to front (pictured). If you're wrapping on the purl side you would bring yarn to the back (not pictured).

Slip the next stitch purlwise.

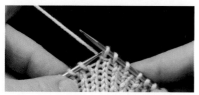

If you're wrapping from the knit side, bring yarn to back (pictured). If you're wrapping from the purl side bring yarn to the front (not pictured).

Slip the stitch back to the left hand needle, then turn work.

Work back in the direction you just came from.

121

Pick up Wrap

When you reach a stitch that has been previously wrapped, slip the stitch, then pick up the wrap with your left hand needle and lift it to the left needle.

Slip the stitch back to the left hand needle.

Knit (or purl) the wrap and the stitch together.

Pick up Gusset

With working yarn in the back, insert a crochet hook through the center of the side stitch.

Pull yarn up through the stitch, making a loop and place on your working needle.

When the correct number of stitches have been picked up, knit as usual forming a corner.

Lazy Daisy

With your tapestry needle come up through the fabric, then go back down through the fabric, coming up at the opposite side of where you want your loop to be placed. Allow your yarn to form a loop around the point of the needle.

Pull the needle through.

Insert the needle down through the fabric on the outside of the loop.

Lazy Daisy stitch.

Stem Stitch

Bring needle up through fabric, then make a stitch through the fabric pointed back toward the origin.

Again make a stitch pointed back toward where you last went through the fabric.

Always keep the needle on the same side of the yarn for a nice twisted look.

Stem Stitch.

Bind off

Pick up stitch to the right of the last stitch on the needle.

Pass the right stitch over the left stitch and off the needle.

One stitch bound off.

One stitch bound off in the middle of a row.

Sewn Bind Off

Thread tapestry needle with the yarn tail to be used for binding off. Bring needle through the first two stitches on the needle purlwise.

Go back through the first stitch only, knitwise.

Drop the first stitch off the needle. Repeat from the beginning until all stitches have been sewn and dropped off.

A bound off edge.

Kitchener Stitch

Using a tapestry needle threaded with the yarn tail, insert the tapestry needle into the first stitch on the front needle knitwise.

Drop the first stitch off the front needle. Then insert the tapestry needle into the next stitch purlwise leaving it on the front needle.

Insert the tapestry needle into the first stitch on the back needle knitwise.

Drop the first stitch off the back needle, then insert the tapestry needle in the next stitch on the back needle purlwise leaving it on the back needle.

Repeat from the beginning until all stitches have been grafted.

Special thanks to all of the yarn vendors who graciously provided the beautiful yarns used for the samples in this book.

Resources

Blue Moon Fiberarts
Socks That Rock
bluemoonfiberarts.com

Chameleon Colorworks
Bambino
chameleoncolorworks.com

Curious Creek
Wasonga
curiouscreek.com

Dye Dreams
Luster Sox
Dream Sox
Comfy Sox
dyedreams.com

Enchanted Knoll
Superwash Sock Yarn
etsy.com/shop.php?user_id=58716

Lisa Souza Dyeworks
Sock!
lisaknit.com

Madeline Tosh
Tosh Sock
madelinetosh.com

Malabrigo
Malabrigo Sock
malabrigoyarn.com

Pagewood Farm
Chugiak
St. Elias
pagewoodfarm.com

Shalimar Yarns
Zoe Sock
shalimaryarns.com

Skacel
Trekking
Trekking Pro Natura
Schoppel Wolle Zauberball
Addi Turbo Needles
skacelknitting.com

Woolen Rabbit
Harmony Sock
thewoolenrabbit.com

Fin